ABC's of Turning Dark Nights into Sunny Days: *a guide to finding your way through crisis*

By

Terra Mar

ISBN-13: 978-0-9819917-1-9
ISBN:-10: 0981991718

Published by Macro Connections Publishing, a division of Macro Connections, LLC. Cover design by Katherin Scott

Table of Contents

Introduction

Several years ago I went through a lengthy health crisis following a stage 3 breast cancer diagnosis. I learned an enormous amount. I was also a practicing hypnotherapist and, as fate would have it, ended up meeting several people who were also in crisis, though for many different reasons.

I wanted to write a book that would reassure the reader that no matter what, you still have power over you. I wrote it as a hands-on, step-by-step guide to using challenges as a springboard to your next stage of personal evolution.

This book is in part the result of my journey and theirs as well as my predilection to want to enjoy life. It's also because as the banking crisis spread, more and more people began to find their lives turned upside down. Sometimes it felt totally random.

A friend who had worked at the same company for 28 years was given a handshake, a lot of good wishes and then laid off. Later that same day I overheard snippets of a random cell phone conversation from a stranger: "You know he was laid off and he's pretty depressed, so if you could call him..."

The economy nosedived, and words that were once reserved for an edge of our society moved into the center of our global mosaic:

Layoffs. "Discouraged" workers. Businesses closing. Foreclosures. Family, friends, neighbors, even cities and states facing bankruptcy...

These past few years have created plenty of dark – and sleepless – nights for a whole lot of us. These are added to the life shocks and endings of all sorts that humans face – such as severe illness, debilitating accidents, death of loved ones, and relationships dissolving.

I knew from my experience and that of my clients that even if we can't stop things from hitting us on the head, we can change how we react to life's shocks, challenges and dramas.

Each of us has the ability to blow the whistle, put up our hand, call in the reserves, name the tune and rewrite the lyrics. We may need some tools for that, or a simple reminder. We may need some guidance to help us find the Wonder Woman or Superman within.

Voila this book, simple enough to be called A,B,C, yet filled with a collective wisdom that I have accessed over years of study and practice. Whether used as a learning tool or a sticky note for your mental fridge, the tips, tools, and activities here are tried, tested, and powerful.

They were designed to give you the self-confidence to make changes you may not even think possible, not yet anyway. These changes can be pragmatic or so vast they guide you to a deep cleanse of old thinking.

At the least, this book can help anyone going through a rough patch to find calm, joy, positivity, and reframe some of the bad stuff we often tell ourselves.

It is intended for anyone curious about how their life might look in Hi Def, 3D, wide screen, and everyone daring enough to answer the challenge.

The unknown is known for testing nerves and bringing on the unanticipated. Could be rough, could be easy. Quien sabe...

But then again, what's life without a little uncertainty?

Suggestions for using this book

This book is a cornucopia of techniques I have studied and used, methodologies used by trained, practicing psychologists and hypnotherapists, and approaches I developed that have worked well for me.

It is my offering via many broad, strong shoulders to anyone in need of a place to lean on.

If a particular chapter heading jumps out at you it will probably be most productive to go directly there. On the other hand I have tried to keep a semblance of moving along a continuum of clarity and growth.

Like all ABC books in this series, each chapter ends with an activity designed as a practical technique or takeaway. How much you personally take from the book will depend in part on how actively you pursue the targeted activities.

If you have ever considered keeping a journal I'd say now would be a good time. Alternately, write scribble or doodle right here. It helps make it your own.

Acknowledgment

I am grateful to many people, places and events for this book. My friends and family knew I could do this book even when I didn't. E, you're the best and my favorite cheerleader. Ginny, you've got an eagle eye, a loving spirit and were a fabulous editor.

Dedication

To the three most important men in my life.

To all the courageous spirits who have been there and come out with a smile and a hand extended to others.

To my Village and the love that keeps it flourishing.

> *"If you have inner peace, the external problems do not affect your deep sense of peace and tranquility. In that state of mind you can deal with situations with calmness and reason, while keeping your inner happiness."*
>
> **HH the Dalai Lama** from the Nobel Lecture, 1989

A is for Anxiety

"The source of anxiety lies in the future. If you can keep the future out of mind, you can forget your worries." **Milan Kundera** (Czech Novelist, Playwright and Poet, b.1929)

One moment there you are minding your own business and then suddenly like the loud snap of a tree branch, it all changes. BAM!

A phone call you hoped you'd never get. A pink slip. A notice of foreclosure. No matter what face it wears it's a monster bearing down at full speed about to rip you apart and smash your world into smithereens. Or at least that's the way it feels.

Bad News is both an emotional assault and a physical hit that profoundly impacts our physiology. As our endocrine system pumps out masses of adrenaline, our heart may pound in our ears, our blood pressure rise to a boil, and our breathing hit hyper speed.

And that's just the moment of impact.

What happens next? And much later? What is each day like when you open your eyes? What happens when you wake in the night?

If you find yourself battling bogey men and demons at random times of night and day, you could probably use some help. Help is not only the stuff of **A**.

This book is designed to support you from A to Z. It is a walking stick on your journey from dark nights into many bright sunny days.

How you cope with the ongoing and recurring emotional demands of a Big Blow is the single most telling measurement of how successful you will be at finding your way out of the dark maze and into your custom-built brighter future.

Onions, strawberries and anxiety

I'd like to start with how to scrape yourself up off the floor after the news hits. Getting Bad News is a head-on collision. Everything after that is a process. Understanding doesn't just stand there in blinding glory and fully present itself. Realizations unfold in layers.

Pain too is revealed in layers, but more like an onion because once cut, there will be tears. Did you know the best way not to cry when your olfactory nerves are upset by an onion is to put a different, strong odor right up to your nose?

Sometimes that's all you can do when a crisis hits. Replace the onion with a strawberry; remember someone who loves you, some moment that filled you with strength, let the tears dry and the nerves settle.

But that's momentary. Recurring bouts of anxiety are a byproduct of crisis. If you've had really Bad News and it *didn't* cause any anxiety either you're deeply in shock or completely medicated.

It is the rare person that can get through a prolonged crisis without getting all too intimate with anxiety. To overcome it, learn your mind and your body's signs.

To thine own anxiety be true...

Anxiety is defined in many ways and at many levels. It can go anywhere from a general feeling of malaise to a clinically defined ongoing state of distress.

Obviously anyone with an anxiety disorder needs to seek the counsel of a qualified health care provider.

This chapter is for those of us responding to a sudden event and periodically experiencing a feeling of dread or stress that manifests physically and emotionally in almost as many ways as there are individuals experiencing it.

Beyond the basic similarities we all share in the fight or flight mechanism the differences in how we experience anxiety and how we cope with it are enormous.

You need to know *your* signs of anxiety. That's the first step.

A place of your own

To get out of the anxiety cycle you have to have some-place to go. You can't just jump off a merry-go-round without a soft place to land. The rest of this chapter presents the tool you need to create that landing pad.

Coping with anxiety begins with a space in your mind, your heart, and the deepest parts of your being where you feel calm. It's anxiety's job to attack that space. Yours is to nurture and protect it.

You will need this haven where you feel safety and tranquility. It will be your harbor as the storms rage and the seas swell. I will ask you to go back to this place of yours many times throughout the book. Let's create it now.

Finding your Naturscape

Take in a few slow, deep breaths, relax your body, and imagine where in Nature you are happiest. Where do you long to be? *More importantly, where do you feel safe and comforted?* Fantasize.

Is it a sandy expanse of white beach with palm trees behind you, a calm ocean and warm sun?

A forest near a meandering stream surrounded by a mix of old growth and fresh leaves?

A meadow filled with wild flowers in bloom, or a peaceful garden filled with fragrance and beauty?

Have I missed your heartscape? Wherever it is, create that place in your mind now. Use your senses to feel the grass under your feet, hear the waves break on the beach, see the colors around you, smell the flowers, touch a tree, or simply know it's all there. Take your time.

You must imagine this place vividly and hold the image in your mind.

This is YOUR place of refuge, safety and nourishment. As you repeatedly go there, feel free to move around and decorate it as you wish. It's yours to do with as you please. For now take note of how this feels in your body. Mark the feelings.

I can't stress enough how important this is. Luxuriate. INDULGE. Stay until you feel WONDERFUL! Keep all else at bay. Feel SAFE and CALM and note your physiology in this state.

Now that you feel fabulous I invite you to become mildly anxious by intent. I know it seems odd, but this is a proven method of coping with anxiety. Before you begin though, make sure you are feeling completely calm. Designate that level of calmness as "zero" on your anxiety scale. Another day it may feel slightly different, but when you are as calm as *you* can be, that's always your 'zero.'

From your zero, imagine something that causes you MILD stress or anxiety like running late for an appointment, being stuck in traffic or not finding your keys. *If anxiety were on a scale of 1 – 10 with 10 being the highest, this should be around a **two**.*

Anxiety workdown

From your place of calm, bring yourself into your slightly anxiety-producing situation. *Notice the changes in your physiology as you move from zero to a two on your anxiety scale.*

Only once you have noted the changes, take a deep breath and go back down to your zero. Find again the pleasures of tranquility and safety in your naturscape.

Now using the same sensed memory repeat exactly what you just did. Again note your physiology changes. Once noted, again return to your zero.

One more time please, exactly as before. If you can't muster much anxiety the third time that's fine too.

Good. That's it for now. Easy, right? But its power is amazing. With some practice you can use it for higher anxiety-producing situations. If you do, go slowly up the scale, one number at a time.

Done regularly this simple practice alone will change your life. If you use it, even if you read no further, you can turn a mind in pieces into a mind at peace.

B is for Beliefs

*"That which hinders your task **is** your task."* **Sanford Meisner** (American actor and influential acting coach who created the Meisner Technique, 1905-1997)

Our belief systems are our navigators. When crisis hits we trust our navigator to get us through. If instead we find ourselves off kilter and off course, we may want to consider giving the navigator an updated GPS.

Once Bad News hits, our belief systems will at least get a good shake-up because the disparity between the world we knew and the newly (dis)ordered world we now inhabit can feel so vast as to seem unbridgeable.

Anguished thoughts and disbelief will cascade in, reflecting the huge assault on our current world view. "This can't be happening to me!" "I don't believe it!" "How could they?"

Disarray may pursue us not only in our waking hours, but in dreams and nightmares as well. This is only natural as we desperately seek direction from our navigator to get us through unknown territory.

The all-important question then is whether our navigator has the right equipment to steer us through.

As mentioned in **A is for Anxiety**, after the initial hit it's all a process, and any onslaught will take time to un-ravel. But we must begin somewhere.

I am suggesting we start by separating the strands of our belief systems. We will feel lost in a world gone askew un-less our navigator has the best and most up-to-date equipment on hand.

When losing is gaining

Susan had gotten a pink slip about a year before we met. After long months of job search, her savings were exhausted and so was she. Susan lived in dread that she might have to declare bankruptcy. It was a 3 a.m. nightmare for her. Sweats. Chills. Panic attacks. Grow-ing up poor, the fear of poverty haunted her.

After enough pain and suffering, she was finally ready to examine her beliefs and fears. We broke it down piece by piece. She looked at her own worst case sce-nario and asked herself what she would truly lose in bankruptcy, other than mounting debt. At the end she realized her biggest loss would be her intense fear of loss. Susan went through bankruptcy and was floored by the unexpected freedom it brought.

Her strength came from her willingness to challenge fundamental beliefs. She had had enough of her old fear-based ones. She opened her own Pandora's Box and let the sun shine into old darkened corners. As worn out beliefs melted away, she replaced them with life-positive ones. Once the process took hold she changed, life changed, and her world was different than she had ever imagined.

I understood Susan only too well. Fear of loss had driven me into more negative corners than I care to remember. Letting go allowed me to stand on my own two feet with a sense of adventure in my heart and a smile on my face.

We disempower fear the day we accept that losses are coming our way and we will be okay anyway.

Where do you fit in?

This was Susan's story, but it is yours and mine when it comes to our beliefs. I didn't ask for my beliefs any more than you asked for yours, but we have clung to them anyway. Beliefs were instilled in me, as in you, by our grown-ups and the people we looked up to, loved, or feared. They included parents, older siblings, teachers, and community leaders.

The statements we accepted were powerful and emotionally-laden. As children we made no distinction if they were negative and accusatory or supportive and loving. We swallowed them unconditionally. Many of them are still part of the tools our navigators use.

How do we get a new GPS and other tools?

You and I may not have been responsible for adopting our beliefs, but we are responsible for keeping them.

It took a raging storm of illness for me to wake up and acknowledge that I held on to my individual beliefs for dear life even when they were outdated, outmoded and destructive. Ultimately I made wonderful life-affirming changes.

Does that make me different from you? Absolutely not! We are often told that we learn to manifest by affirmation and by believing we can. Ridiculous!

We are all already perfect manifesters! We're human; it's what we do.

What matters is the degree of absolute clarity about what we want to manifest. We manifest all right, so watch out!

Most of the time most of us manifest the confusion, mush, negativity and fear that reaches up from our subconscious mind and forms the outermost boundaries of our dearly held belief systems.

All too often fear and negative beliefs cancel out our heart's desire. We cannot see ourselves as strong while holding on to old belief that tells us we are weak. We do not manifest wishes. We will not manifest what we believe we cannot accomplish. And we will not ever manifest an affirmation just because we say it. What we will manifest is this: *our dominant belief.*

Those who believe heart and soul in abundance manifest it. Those who believe with undying passion that they deserve love, get it. Those who know with crystal clear certainty that they will travel, be famous, sky dive or own a company will.

Sound simple? From *"Think and Grow Rich"* to *"The Secret"* folks have been telling us to just do it.

Why haven't more of us 'just done' it?

Simply put, because we don't take the time, mental space, energy, and consistency to get the clarity we need and then change any beliefs that impede us.

We are constantly tempted to go for quick and easy solutions and away from quiet time. Our inner life is not validated and our outer selves are quickly judged. We ignore the profound connection to our inner nature, which would actually make the task easy. But you can change your beliefs, and I will show you how.

Beliefativities

❖ First, find one belief or one component of your belief system that has caused you grief, hardship, trouble or in some way has not done well by you. Write that sucker down! Fessing up is the first step in change.

No one else has to see it, but you have to spill the beans. You can write it elsewhere, but I recommend you write it right here, right now.

_____

_____

_____

❖ If you didn't find an inner haven in the **A** activity, please do it now. BTW, if you didn't, I invite you to examine the belief that managed to stop you.

Go to your naturscape the same way as in **A**. Make it more yours by adding something, walking around or playing. Stay calm, and feel completely safe.

Now bring in that belief. Talk to it. Yell at it if you want. Cajole it into serving you. Whatever strikes your fancy is likely to be the best approach. By the way, I'm pretty auditory. Use whatever sense is most dominant for you. Especially in the beginning give yourself a while for this, and for heaven's sake DON'T QUESTION IT!

Listen/see/feel, etc. whatever comes and accept it with gratitude. Whatever happens or doesn't happen is good for now. If it's the latter, come back another time. If that doesn't work, consider seeking help to change that stubborn belief.

C is for Crisis

"Character cannot be developed in ease and quiet. Only through experiences of trial and suffering can the soul be strengthened, vision cleared, ambition inspired and success achieved." **Helen Keller** (American author and educator who was blind and deaf 1880-1968)

OK, the world as you knew it came crashing down. You have scraped yourself off the floor and perhaps have even begun to examine beliefs that do not serve you. Your current life is still One Big Crisis. Now what? How do you take that and shape it into the life you want?

Here's how: step by step, layer by layer.

Step number one is SLOW DOWN! If it's really a crisis and not a drama-of-the-day you will NOT resolve it overnight.

Perhaps you've heard this piece of wisdom that has become a western business and New Age cliché: Two Chinese characters come together to form the word crisis. They are 'danger' and 'opportunity.' This has been strenuously debunked by Chinese scholars.

Apparently most mother tongue Chinese consider it wishful and naïve thinking. The view prevails that crisis calls instead for maturity, acceptance, and restraint. Most crises entail loss and hardship, so suck it up, cut your losses, and move on. I say: Crap!

A crisis is indeed the conjunction of danger and opportunity, at least in English. The online *ask.com* dictionary, similar to Webster and others defines crisis this way:

a) Crucial or decisive point or situation; *a turning point.* (italics added)

b) Unstable condition... involving an impending abrupt or decisive change.

c) Emotionally stressful event or traumatic change in a person's life.

d) Point in a story or drama when a conflict reaches its highest tension and must be resolved.

Wishful thinking?

Consider the definition. Life has us on the precipice. Change is inevitable. Unlike the Zen tale of the guy caught between a tiger chasing him off a cliff and a tiger waiting below to eat him as two mice chew away on his only handhold, the outcome for us on the edge is not so easily foretold.

Even the victim of the Zen morality tale picks a strawberry and is transported by its absolute deliciousness.

Even facing an inevitable outcome we still have a choice. We still have the opportunity to experience life at its fullest. Even in the midst of crisis, we still get to choose who we are as we go through the experience.

We can move back the line that crosses us into the danger zone. We can decide to revel in new, unexpected opportunities. By redefining what we consider both danger and opportunity, we take the first step in transforming the dark nights of crisis into bright, sunny days.

Refusing to acknowledge the opportunity in a crisis is blindly living in denial. According to Thomas Moore, psychologist and author of *"Dark Nights of the Soul,"* during crisis we swim around in an "alchemical barrel." In there we can mature into fine wine or turn sour like vinegar. The choice *is* ours.

Undoubtedly post-crisis we will end up changed – for better or worse. The good news is that we get to choose which it will be.

While it may take a village to help us through a crisis (check out **V**), those of us in the crisis are the only ones who can rise up to meet it. Accepting that additional burden of responsibility on top of a Big Hit may not be easy, but it is a major step in finding our way through.

Who shall I choose to be?

When I began the laborious process of figuring out my options following a stage 3 breast cancer diagnosis, which I think by anyone's definition is a crisis, I relied on my sister's wise words.

She had received her own cancer diagnosis years before and told me I needed to decide who I would be going through it. Mulling that over called out all my courage and role model instincts.

I opted to be a model for my family, for those who would be diagnosed after me, and for myself. That last was the most arduous because it entailed truly facing my fears, not acting 'as if' to others.

Although I didn't always meet my expectations, at least I had them. I apparently did serve as a model to many, including my Naturopath who told me that she went on a three-day 60 mile walk-for-a-cure.

It rained for two of those days, and often she was miserable. The worst was when her shoes were wet and rubbing against calluses, and her feet bled. At those moments she thought of me, and took another step forward.

Crisis: danger and opportunity. The danger is obvious. It's finding the opportunity – and the struggle to live it – that makes us whole.

Crisativities

❖ Once again, please go back to the naturscape you created in **A**. A few deep breaths and focus is all the transportation you need.

❖ If this is your first really Big Crisis, once in your naturscape, break it down into its component parts. Make the pieces as small as possible. Now

16

imagine yourself getting all the help you need in your heartscape. Send yourself forward in time and imagine yourself emerging stronger and happier from every aspect of the crisis you are currently experiencing.

❖ For the rest of us: Before this Big One, recall a crisis you went through. Did you find an opportunity in it? Were you changed for the better? *If so*, once in your naturscape call up those wonderful images of courage and wisdom, of calm acceptance and creative change. **Bask in each and every one!**

❖ *If not*, go back there and change it now. Insist on a do-over! Be your own advocate. Feel the power as you change your past and create a new outcome. Transfer that power to your current situation.

Whichever path you took -- Bravo! Now you can smile about the changes you made!

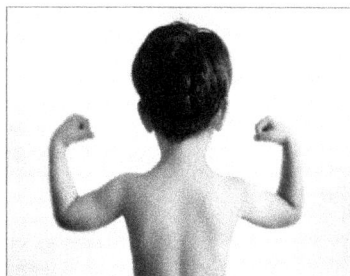

D is for Dream

"...the work goes on, the cause endures, the hope still lives, and the dream shall never die." The late **Senator Edward M. Kennedy** (1932-2009)

We live according to our beliefs, our myths, and our dreams. When a Big Crisis hits, our beliefs are assaulted as we cling desperately to our myths. And our dreams, what happens to our dreams?

They are shattered. They are literally torn out of our souls and trampled on by a financial, health, housing, relationship or other loss.

Janet came to me in the early stages of a protracted legal and financial crisis. Explaining what motivated her to see me, Janet said it all began at a traffic light. Stopped at red, she suddenly felt completely drained, as if putting her foot on the gas would be impossible. As the moment passed she realized she felt burdened, trapped, and plain worn out.

Then she started thinking of her life as a metaphorical traffic light that only had red, no orange, and no green.

Only then did she get that she was depressed, seriously depressed. This was a condition unusual enough for Janet that it took her a while to get the symptoms.

She realized her crisis impacted almost every area of her life expanding beyond financial and legal concerns into social life for her and her family, school for her children, and on and on. It would not take much digging to figure out why she was depressed.

Women at the well

Oddly enough, once the exploration was underway what Janet discovered was none of the above. Well not directly anyway. It was her dreams. *Her dreams had come crashing down and she had no new ones to put in their place. She didn't dare.*

Janet was sensitive and intuitive. She had always gone to her dreams like women to a well. She slowly became aware of how much life-sustaining hope she had always gathered from dreaming.

One day she explained that her husband worried whenever she began a sentence with: *"So…"*

He knew from years of walks and drives, road trips and evenings after the kids were in bed that he was about to hear the latest dream. First came "so," and then Janet dreamed out loud.

"So, what if we pack up the kids and drive to Mexico?"

"So, what do you think about building a house out of mud and clay?"

"So, what if we move to Europe and start a B & B?"

On it went over the years and the decades. Life always had a section marked 'realm of the possible.' There Janet nurtured a clean slate, her tabula rasa.

Now for the first time she could remember, life had stolen her dreams. Damn. Damn, damn. Nothing could have depressed her more.

Janet understood what many of us have still to learn: She had a fierce certainty that she could neither cope nor heal without reclaiming dreaming. Not the old dreams, they were OBE (overtaken by events). She had but one choice; she had to find new dreams.

Reclaiming the dream, the dream, the dream...

In hard times, while it is essential to stay connected to the present moment, it is equally essential that we take time out and dream.

It wasn't easy for Janet. Not only had she never before had such a Big crisis. She had difficulty understanding how to recapture dreaming in the midst of the very crisis that had stolen her ability to dream. Here is what we did.

I offered two tools that helped guide Janet to reclaim dreaming, find new dreams, and infuse her with a renewed sense of empowerment. They are available to anyone willing to jump over their own shadows and use them: *Gratitude and trust.*

Gratitude:

I asked her to get a small diary size journal, about 4 x 6. That way I knew she wouldn't get lost in expectations of having to fill a big book. Every day for months she wrote what she was grateful for.

Starting may be tough, but once you grab on to a few threads and put them in writing the list easily grows.

I also asked her to write what she will be grateful for in the future. There are a lot of ways to do this. You can write what you will be grateful for by evening or the weekend, in a month or a year. It can be what you'll be grateful for after a certain event, or undefined by time, what you'll be grateful for once you have it.

That last one is big medicine because to find out what you will be grateful for in the future you have to dream a wonderful future.

I recommend putting all gratitude statements in the present tense, no matter where they are in time, even if it feels a little tortuous.

Enter trust

Gratitude during crisis may seem a stretch; in which case trust may feel more like a living, breathing oxymoron. For starters, we need to trust that we are not crazy to dare dream a future that will be wonderful.

At a time when planning life even a month ahead may be difficult you may be surprised at how the gratitude process builds trust. It is exhilarating to see patterns emerge as you write week after week.

Gratitude repeated both creates dreams and makes manifest our strongly held desires. With trust, these turn into deeply held beliefs. Such beliefs, forged in gratitude and trust, are the most powerful form of dreaming into existence a changed reality.

By the way, I'm calling it dreaming because of the myths I live by. You may prefer to call it prayer.

Dreamativities

❖ What happened to your dreams when the Big One hit? Did they crash and burn in an instant? Are they perhaps hanging on to your inner life by a thread?

Take a moment and go to your safe place. Once you feel calm and wonderful, recall a dream you once had. Pick it up and dust if off. Now how does it look, feel, sound etc.? Is it outdated or is it still vibrant?

If you like what you found, be grateful. Find a way to express your gratitude and bring the good feelings back with you when you return.

❖ If you can't get excited at that dream, go out on a limb and pick a new super huge mega oversized Big Dream. Feel it intensely. Use as many of your senses as possible to create strong emotions. Hang on to it and keep it close even once you're back from your inner world.

❖ At your leisure, do this dreamativity again. Repeat. Repeat. Repeat. Same dream, new dreams. Repeat. Repeat. Repeat.

E is for Elegance

"I began to see the character more as a metaphor for how a person survives and manages to maintain his innocence. I just love the bravery and elegance with which he faces the violence in the world." **Neil Jordan** (Irish director. His films include 'The Crying Game' and 'Interview with the Vampire')

In Rio de Janeiro I met a doctor who worked as a pediatrician in a large hospital. Over and over she saw the same life-threatening illnesses among the children. Far too often children she had helped cure came back with the same illness. Frequently they returned sicker than the first time as their immune systems declined.

The pattern was clear. She was sending children right back into the conditions that had caused severe illnesses in the first place: unsanitary conditions, improper nutrition, and no money for medicines.

Elegance in Rio

She knew the children were from poor homes and decided to look at their living situations for herself. The results were historic for health care throughout Brazil. Dr. Cordeiro (http://www.ashoka.org/Vera_Cordeiro) began a non-profit organization that has become a model of care in many hospitals in Brazil.

Renascer (Rebirth) connects families with social workers, nurses, doctors, businesses and government agencies. The goal is simple and quantifiable. Stay with the family as long as it takes to change the underlying conditions of illness. Renascer ensures that severely ill impoverished children receive fully integrated care from the ground up.

One afternoon we talked about what motivated her to exchange her career for a non-profit organization. She said she knew the children were poor, but had no idea of their lives until she saw where they lived.

Mothers came to her wearing good dresses, jewelry, and make-up. From the way they looked and handled themselves she could not guess how destitute they were. She had no idea that friends and neighbors lent mothers what they needed for the doctor's visit.

Their lives could hardly be filled with more suffering: They lived in dire poverty with a severely, often terminally, ill child. These were women from whom so much had been taken. But their dignity remained, as did their inherent elegance.

Life rafts

Crisis can take away many things, but only we can give away our elegance. I like the word because it conjures up images of beauty in the midst of plenty. We use it to describe something or someone that seems to personify grace, refinement, and good taste. Aesthetic pleasures surround the word. Slip into a silk blouse or shirt. Elegant. Sip Dom Perignon champagne. Elegant.

When we keep our elegance we are holding onto two life rafts at once: the feeling that we are deserving of good, and our innate human dignity.

These are the opposite of original sin. They are an inner cleanliness. These life rafts brook no 'because' and no qualifiers. They are inherent. Just because we are, they are.

We desperately need them in the choppy waters of crisis – especially as time goes by and we are in danger of getting worn out, worn down, and accepting that we are less than we had once believed.

That's why I'm talking about *keeping* our elegance, not going out and finding it. It's in there. All I'm suggesting is that we bring those feelings into our awareness so we make sure to keep what is rightly ours.

The moments we remember that part of ourselves, we feel better and stand taller. In that state we may also recall the times in our lives when we felt graced and blessed.

There's another meaning to elegance that I like. That's the one we refer to in evaluating solutions to difficult and thorny issues, from the mathematical to the social. A streamlined, simple, precise solution is aka *elegant*.

Remembering elegance in our demeanor, elegance in our thoughts, and elegance in our solutions may not be easy. But it's a good challenge, and one we can choose to take on each day.

You may have your own ways to feel elegant, and there are any number of small acts to remind ourselves of our innate elegance. Here are a few of mine:

Elegantivities

❖ One day as you run an errand dress up. Accessorize. Notice any difference?

❖ Go through your closet. Anything that makes you feel uncomfortable? Old? Fat? Ugly? GET RID OF IT!

❖ Wash your sheets more often. Put lavender on your pillow. Feel elegant as you slip into bed.

❖ Clean the refrigerator, use aromatherapy, take a bubble bath...

F is for Frantic

Leslie: *"I can't believe the two of you are eating in the middle of a crisis like this".*
Gary: *"We're nervous, what do you want."*
Leslie: *"Then take a Valium like a normal person."*
Dialogue from the film '**Desperately Seeking Susan**' (1985)

Don't be surprised if you sometimes feel frantic as you deal with the Big One. Feeling frantic may even hold a bizarre sense of comfort if it is a known quantity. It may give you a sense that you are doing something even if you can't control the Big Stuff coming your way.

Don told me he felt that way. He said part of what made him feel frantic was the quiet in his life. There were storms raging on every front – health, money, relationships, future plans spiraling down the drain… yet life in the storm's eye was quiet. Bright, sunny, and startlingly silent.

No one was knocking down the door, no one tried to haul him off to debtor's prison. He lived with the expectation that sooner or later those raging storms would reach his door and tear it down.

The disconnect was enormous, and Don went so far as to question his sanity. The sun was coming up every morning and the moon at night. Mondays gave way to

Tuesdays; he still took showers and ate lunch. He cracked jokes, laughed, and went out with friends.

But then what we dubbed 'the frantics' snuck up on him. The frantics was insidious because Don's inner turmoil was hidden to the outside world and often even he mistook it.

The deep frantics

He was living part of his life in a hidden mental rut that was often not even conscious. He was living on an endless merry-go-round (hold the merry) of the same problems, same options, same attempts at resolution, same doors slamming, over and over, round and round. The last thing at night and the first thing in the morning.

It often came on suddenly with no immediate event to precipitate it, and no warning. How could this be fixed? What will life be in a month or six? How will I survive this mess? He lived with an ongoing refrain that had no melody, only echoes.

That was *not* insanity; that was frantic for Don. Like anxiety, frantic is unique to each of us going through it. Like anxiety, we need to know our own version. His defied the active, chicken without a head frantic. He could be chatting with someone or doing a task, appearing quite normal. At the same time in a deep and inescapable level Don was living the frantics.

We agreed he needed to do something about it and if you've got the frantics, I'd urge you to as well.

Deep six the frantics

Unlike openly recognizable frantic behavior the frantics is insidious because it's all so quiet. It's under the surface, which makes it possible to avoid. But the frantics will eat you for lunch. It will wear you down; use you up, spit you out and leave you not only exhausted, but way the worse for wear.

If we keep living with the frantics it changes nothing -- except us. We change physiologically, spiritually, and emotionally and it's all a loss for us and a win for the frantics.

If you recognize the syndrome you'll be happy to hear there are antidotes to that poison. There's **Defogging**, **Triple Hitter**, and **Breath**.

Defogging

First acknowledge that the frantics is a manifestation of some fear. No way can we stop the fear if we deny its existence.

It's okay to fool others. In fact sometimes, as in modeling for others, I'm in favor of it. To fool ourselves is a one way journey to hell.

Your crisis is an opportunity for you to strip bare right down to your muscles, bones, molecules and DNA. The first step in ensuring you don't get into the same crisis again is a deep and consistent level of honesty with Number One. Make it so.

Drag those bogeymen out of their cobwebbed corners and into the light. Tell a trusted friend of your fears, of how you feel when you are frantic. Expose the demon and watch it disappear like fog lifting under the strong rays of the sun.

I don't think I can overemphasize this point. It is a sine qua non of coping positively and of healing.

Triple Hitter

Remember as a kid you needed to learn how to stop, look and listen before crossing a street? This is similar, and it also takes practice.

Stop, ask, and listen

Once we acknowledge that we are afraid, it is time to take a break and **S-T-O-P**. This is not a time for judgments. It's time to really stop. I don't mean stop feeling frantic, that will come. I mean stop the mind from running roughshod over you by talking to yourself.

A-S-K. *Take control by talking to yourself and insist that you get an answer.* Ask questions like "What is my biggest fear?"

L-I-S-T-E-N for the answer. Make one up if it doesn't come. It doesn't matter if it wells up or if you pull it out of thin air. It's still you doing the pulling, so you can work with that.

I repeat this is *not* the time for judgments. Accept what you get and move on to the next question, such as: "What is the worst that could happen?"

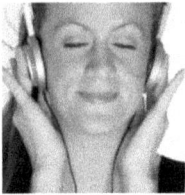

Keep at it. A good technique is to keep asking *"And then?"* WAIT for the answer. *And then?* WAIT for the answer. *And then?* Continue to WAIT for the answer until you've reached a dead end.

You may be amazed at how freeing this is. It's the equivalent of turning and facing the monster in a dream. Generally that awful ogre will wither and become harmless in the face of your presence. So too with the waking monsters.

Breath

Breathe.

I mean this in the sense of the great spiritual, religious, and yogic teachings that have endured throughout the ages and been passed on to us.

The underlying assumption is simple: Control your breathing and you control your life.

When our body goes into panic mode the first thing we lose is slow easy breathing. It is enormously helpful to become aware of our bodies and our breath during tough times.

Taking a yoga class to help you with deep breathing is a great option. Signing up for a meditation class can help if you trust the teacher and the method.

Even whenever you think about it during the day just taking some deep, slow breaths is refreshing, beneficial, and an excellent reminder.

Even better though if you are able, is to add a 10-minute meditation during the day. Use your mind to follow the breath, or more accurately keep pulling your mind back to follow the breath. This can help to calm your breathing and gently tame your runaway mind.

Franativities

❖ Go to your naturscape, your inner place of calm and safety you created in **A**. From that comfortable place call up *one* of your worries. Give it some form -- human, animal or symbolic. You are about to enter into a discussion with it.

Use the stop, ask and listen technique mentioned above. Make sure you continue with *"and then"* until you find a sense of completion.

Take all the time you need to soothe and calm yourself before you come back.

❖ If you feel yourself getting frantic, find the physical location in your body where it is.

Breathe into that place and keep at it until that spot softens, lightens, or relaxes. Use any additional calming techniques in your tool box.

❖ Either when you feel frantic or any other time you have an opportunity, consider **G.**

The next chapter can help with gratitude for what you have right now at this very moment as you gently pull yourself into the here and now.

G is for Gratitude

"Gratitude is one of the least articulate emotions, especially when it is deep" **Felix Frankfurter** (American Jurist, 1882-1965)

If we were perfect beings we would have no impetus to try to understand gratitude. Sans suffering and stress there would be no need for gratitude as a spiritual practice. But of course there is both impetus and need, which is why throughout the ages we humans have been mulling over the role of gratitude in our lives.

The practice of gratitude is a cornerstone of right living in every religious, spiritual, mystical and metaphysical tradition. Any belief system that entails prayer in its largest sense also recommends gratitude.

Something that important should be deserving of our focus and in-depth consideration, yet too few of us stop to consider what gratitude really is.

As a palliative against the ills of the world, gratitude is recommended to help us reframe and overcome the negative dramas of our individual lives. It is invoked by survivors of life threatening accidents and illnesses, and those who have suffered through trials and tribulations of all kinds.

Gratitude after the fact

As common as is the call to gratitude, it is most frequently invoked after the fact. We tend to fill in the gratitude blanks as part of a euphoric afterglow of surviving something Bad as in: "Aah how grateful I am that I didn't drown when I fell into the river."

Using gratitude in this way is tantamount to the wish of a child who cheats on a test when suddenly the teacher gets up from behind the desk: 'If I don't get caught cheating I swear I'll never, ever look at anyone else's answers again.' True to Mae West's adage about resisting anything but temptation, such prayers are easy to keep until the next time.

My after the fact gratitude was about recovering from cancer. I was profoundly grateful and made sincere promises. With time I felt the shifts in my life, and knew I was becoming forgetful. Eventually I learned that I was temporarily negotiating gratitude rather than living it.

Humans have an astounding ability to forget, and time really does heal. As trauma recedes, post-facto gratitude slips away with it. Life changes, things get better, we move on.

There is an alternative that is surprisingly easy. It is the intentional practice of living in gratitude as a state of heart and mind.

In the traditional Japanese martial art I practiced for decades, upon arriving at the dojo we bowed. As we left we bowed. I experienced this as a way of clearing outside influences upon entering the training area and appreciation for the training I had received as I left.

One day my teacher spoke at length about the many layers of "re," the Japanese bow. He discussed the power of gratitude and said "all training begins and ends with gratitude." It took me years to appreciate the wisdom of his words.

Don't think about pastries

I spent time in Vienna, a place known throughout the world for its coffee houses. They are wonderful, and there are a lot of them, but Vienna's best desserts are found in bakeries, and those are ubiquitous.

I liked Vienna's bakeries way too much. When I wanted a sweet and when I wanted to avoid one, bakeries began to surround me. Then there were the other times I didn't even smell a bakery no less see one.

Those were the uncommon moments that I was truly *indifferent*. Not wanting or wanting had exactly the same effect: sudden, frequent bakery appearances. Only true indifference kept them at bay and me Danish free.

WOW! I could avoid carbs not by willing them out of existence, but by ignoring their existence! From a purely practical perspective I was delighted at the power of my thoughts. I could create negative hallucinations!

Granted sometimes it was more like 'don't think about elephants' and bakeries appeared on cue in all their tempting glory. But that was mostly in the beginning when I wanted to cheat here and there anyway.

After some trial, error and cherry Danish, I realized that I could use the power of intentional focus to change the world around me. So can you.

It would sound crass and out of touch were I to suggest you could fix your affairs by ignoring the existence of the biggest mess you've ever been in. That's not going to happen. I know that if you're in a crisis it's close to impossible to avoid thinking about it.

How to outsmart your crisis

If you have the personality to use indifference, go for it because it is empowering. I found another approach to change my focus. I liked it better than indifference because it acknowledged a natural tendency to worry, fret and dote.

I discovered that regular intentional doses of gratitude reframed the world around me. It battled troubles by renaming, reframing and reclaiming.

This was not gratitude after the fact. It was not event focused nor related to downs, ups, or the blahs. This was a way of viewing and molding the world.

If you want monumental change and prayer doesn't seem to move the mountain, try gratitude! I know many techniques for finding strength and positivity, but gratitude is in a class by itself.

If you want to try it out, feel free to begin small. You can even start with "I'm grateful that my life is in the garbage can because…" and then force an answer. At the very least it may get you a smile. It might even open a door.

If nothing comes as you seek a moment of gratitude, be grateful your brain cells are functioning and allowing you to search. Be grateful. Be grateful for making the effort to be grateful. Don't give up, keep at it.

The astounding thing with gratitude is how after a while stuff bubbles up seemingly out of nowhere. Even from the depths of self-pity you may remember something for which you are grateful.

Before you know it you're back on track and likely to feel grateful that you persevered and reclaimed your best intentions.

More food for gratitude

In addition to coffee and pastries, in Vienna bread and beer are two other major food groups. Continuing with food for grateful thinking, consider yeast.

If we think of yeast as gratitude, it uplifts heavy flour and changes the chemical structure of a watery brew until it is ready to become a glass of the cold one.

For this delightful alchemy to occur, yeast needs the right atmosphere -- warmth and sugar. Gratitude needs sincere intent. With it, gratitude is expansive and an inevitable source of transformation.

My martial art begins and ends with gratitude. As an intentional practice beginning and ending a moment, a day, a year or a life with gratitude is transformational.

It doesn't need to be focused on something huge like getting through cancer or not drowning in a river. Because gratitude itself is vast, the object of it can be small, even teensy. Gratitude just needs to be, often.

If you feel gratitude for sun shining through leaves, or a good meal, or a smile -- then you've got the sugar going, and the alchemy of change has already begun.

Practiced often gratitude turns waves of okayness into tsunamis of happiness. It geometrically increases our power beyond mere coping and helps us create the world of our choosing.

When it comes to gratitude Nike got it right. Just do it! Nevertheless, a few techniques and supports may be welcome.

Gratativities

❖ Consider making, finding or getting a gratitude bowl or box. Fill it. Designate a tree you love as your gratitude tree. Tie on little notes of gratitude Turn this book into a gratitude spot. Fill in spaces with notes of gratitude.

❖ Keep a gratitude journal. Specifics are in the chapter **D is for Dreams.**

❖ Remember how grateful you were for something that came your way. Consider telling that person directly or writing it down.

❖ Consider paying gratitude forward. Offer a random act known only to you for which some person may be grateful.

H is for Hope

"Hope is the thing with feathers that perches in the soul, and sings the tune without words, and never stops at all." **Emily Dickinson** (American Poet, 1830-1886)

If you were bitten by a deadly snake while carrying an antidote to the venom, would you hesitate to inject it? Would you refuse water if you were lost in a desert?

I'm crazy for even asking, right?

By not daring to hope when life seems to have us by the throat, we do the spiritual and emotional equivalent. We know our bodies die if denied essential needs.

So what's our problem with feeling dumb if we hang on to hope when things look bad?

If our emotional life and our spirit were a physical body that required sustenance we would easily understand the inherent dangers of starving it.

Our dreams feed that body. Gratitude feeds it. And hope does as well. These are as vital to our emotional and spiritual body as an antidote or a drink of water to our physical ones.

There are people who easily maintain hope; I live with one. This chapter is for the rest of us.

Stay, sweet platitude

I'll resist the urge to say something as clichéd and simplistic as hang on to hope even in the harshest of times. Instead I'd like to consider what happens when we let it go.

Blindsided by Big Troubles, hope can be considered just more collateral damage. Sometimes it feels a lot easier to cut the line and let 'er sink.

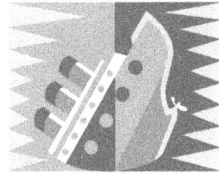

Here's the problem. It's like opening a door and finding nothing on the other side. We may find ourselves in such a dark place that we just keep falling. Or we may bump into our worst fears and nightmares in the dark.

Whichever it is we're defenseless because of this simple reality -- the emotionally sustaining lights go out the moment we let go of this elusive little guy.

Let's say we acknowledge how important it is to keep on hoping, and don't want to give it up. How do we hang on when we're tired, worn down and frazzled?

Simply put: *suck it up and fight off the demons.*

Bet you were hoping for something easier, but it's not as hard as it may sound. Still, like a lot of life's goodies it does take some practice.

When I was journeying through cancer treatment the thing I felt the least control over was other people and what they might say. It pulled the rug out from under me more often than anything else.

I don't know what ridiculous switch it is in people that make them think 'ah, cancer patient... need to tell my favorite cancer horror story.' For most of us on the receiving end it's an unexpected package of all our fears and anxieties offered up as a mirror. Sometimes it took my breath away.

Maybe not everyone going through cancer was as vulnerable, but I had to learn to shake off those unexpected hair-raisers. What taunted me was not really the words but the reverberations they created, the echoes of my own fears.

Echoes through the canyons

Fear is the single largest and most persistent barrier to hope.

I could listen to those fear-filled echoes over and over. I could keep replaying the scary words until they became my own, and then add them to a growing litany of frightening possibilities. I could stick with the known and suffer.

My only other choice was to dare take that first big step into the unknown.

Like you, I am most comfortable with what is familiar -- helpful or not. I didn't like my options, but I had a choice, as do you.

It might help if you remind yourself as I did: *Fear is the single largest and most persistent barrier to hope.*

My light switch

I found a way through the labyrinthine mindset of echoes. It was a phrase I was given by a cancer care professional. I found it adaptable to any fear-based situation. It became one of the most healing mantras I ever learned.

Especially in the beginning it took great intent for me to make the behavior change. That's the sucking up part. If I didn't want to live so fear-based I was going to have to learn something new.

I had to take a step back and understand that statistics were only statistics, they weren't me. I had to learn that what happened to someone else did not have to happen to me. I had to understand that even if it or something worse happened, as long as I had a life I wanted it to be a good one.

I was lucky to be offered some deceptively simple phrases and I'm happy to pay them forward.

"That's his story, it's not my story. That's her story, it's not my story."

Those words held for me the magic of creation. They left me free to create my own story.

No longer was my only option to accept what I had been handed. I had a way to create the positive thoughts, positive images, imagined steps and the outcomes I wanted for myself. It gave me a tool to combat fear no matter what others said. It gave me, well in a word, it gave me hope.

Hope is not as intangible as we may think

Imagine back to when you were watching your favorite sport, or American Idol or the Oscars. You had grand 'hope' for your favorite. The experience was exciting, nerve-wracking, and intense. It was good fun, albeit superficial in that it wasn't your life. Still it served a great purpose.

It identified in your body the *physiology* of hope.

Just thinking about it, we can easily recall the flutter, the smile, the intensity, maybe yelling or biting our nails. We can remember the moment we knew our choice would win and our eyes got bigger or dewy, or we threw a victory sign up in the air. Whew! Intense. Saweeet!

When we're in there rooting for the home team, hope is not abstract. It's bursting with the physiology of emotional intensity.

Once we turn off the TV, we need to look at how to carve hope out of nothing but our own intent.

An easy way to strengthen the connection between intent and hope is to reconnect with the physiology and emotions we had when the TV was on and we hoped for a win. Once we recreate it physiologically, it's already ours.

P.S. on the physiology of hope

If you allow your body to experience the physiological positivity of hope, you may notice it places you in the same physiological state as joy and gratitude.

It's vastly more profound than a change of mind.

It is literally a change in our brainwaves. Done often enough, it creates new neural pathways, and as that process occurs we change.

The improbable becomes likely. The unthinkable becomes possible. And our dreams, once shattered, begin to take a renewed luster and vibrant shape.

In my view of the world, hope is as essential as a beating heart.

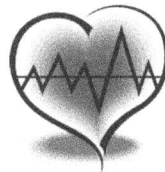

Hopeativities

❖ Bring up a simple image that gives you your version of the warm fuzzies --something like holding a baby or playing with a puppy. Feel the shift in your physiology.

Keep at it till you feel a smile on your face.

Focus now on your heart. Feel how it gets warmer or bigger or lighter. Stay there because that's incorporating your own physiology of hope.

❖ Imagine something you really wanted – *and got*. Taste, smell, feel, see, and emote all over that victory. Make it a part of you.

❖ Now pull off *one small part* of your current crisis. Dream yourself an ideal resolution. Take it with you and move into the heartscape you created in **A**.

Feel how safe you are at this very moment and then apply the outcome you created. Not as a hope now, but as a done deal.

That's good. That's enough.

I is for Isolation

"...I am involved in Mankind; and therefore never send to know for whom the bell tolls; It tolls for thee." Meditation XVII **John Donne** (English clergy, poet 1572 - 1631)

Isolation in a health context means separation from others so no harm comes from or to you. Events viewed in isolation help us interpret the world around us. But what about those who are coping with crisis?

Self-imposed isolation can feel like a sensible choice. Especially in a publicly available crisis like foreclosure or bankruptcy, shame and blame may take hold and the desire for isolation is likely to follow.

Tom lived in a small town and had a high-profile job for the county. He was accused of sexually harassing a female coworker and faced not only financial and legal difficulties, but lots of small-town publicity. As his legal drama dragged on each nuance was cause for a minor media storm.

Cocooning

He needed to protect himself in a town that had one movie theater, only a few restaurants and two supermarkets. He stood little chance of going anywhere without bumping into someone who knew him.

His response was to spin a cocoon around himself whenever he went out. Over time he found himself trapped there. The peering eyes of the outside world couldn't pierce the thick weave, but neither could much else.

Exactly when he needed the support of loved ones, he found it impossible to reach beyond his own self-imposed isolation.

It seemed great at first, but it was a bargain with the devil. The cocoon's safety helped with coping, but hindered his ability to get help and to heal.

Protection that has no off switch is not a sustainable coping mechanism. It is a personally designed prison.

There is no "C" on your forehead

Illness can engender a sense of isolation, especially a 'public' one, if we feel we look different. During chemo I covered my head when I went out. I sometimes felt so isolated from the (apparently) healthy world around me that I felt like I had a 'C' branded on my forehead instead of a pretty scarf on top of it.

Without realizing I spent a lot of time scanning for other women wearing scarves hoping to find someone who looked like me. That state of mind helped me cope for a while, but it would never let me heal.

Every time I used my I-am-Other cocoon I inadvertently isolated myself from my support system. My family, friends, co-workers, associates, and a fabulous healing team were at the ready. Yet I frequently denied myself those healing resources in exchange for self-imposed isolation.

As Tom's legal crisis and financial stresses bore down, his isolation mutated from a coping mechanism into an integral part of who he was becoming through his ordeal. His marriage was beginning to crumble.

To regain his personal power Tom would have to redefine self-protection and be willing to emerge from his cocoon. That turned out to be the biggest battle. Tom said he felt like an addict struggling against the urge for a quick fix as he sought to deny himself the relief of isolation.

A cloak instead

Prison or no, his cocoon had come to represent comfort and safety. Before he could find better coping mechanisms he had to believe that despite the goodies, the price on this one was way too high.

Once he decided to accept a form of protection that he wouldn't always use we had fun creating more subtle and appropriate means of protective gear. Feeling safe but more open he was able to begin strengthening his marriage and reap the benefits of support and counsel of trusted friends.

I told Tom about a mental image I used to stop feeling like I was branded with a 'C'. I introduced him to the magic cloak I kept with me and could throw around me at will on a moment's notice.

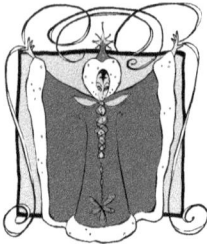

That metaphor helped change my thinking, behavior, and emotional responses to the outside world as I journeyed through my own public challenges.

By nature I am not internalized, detached, or insulated, and sometimes these traits come in handy. So I sewed them into the lining of my cloak. That way I had them instantly as I elegantly slipped on my mantle.

Unlike a Klingon cloaking device, my robe was not intended to make me invisible. At home it rested on a hook. As I ventured into the uncertain outside world I wrapped it around me like a beautiful adornment.

I balanced my desire for protection with the ability to step into community. I knew if necessary I could always conjure my cloak and calmly fiddle with the pleats.

Tom created his mantle in the same way I suggest you design yours here below. Not too long after that, the same woman accused another man of sexual harassment. He discovered that she had done this before in a different state and won a huge settlement. He counter-sued and won.

All claims against Tom were dropped and he was reinstated with back pay. One month later he gave notice, having received a better offer elsewhere.

Cloakativities

❖ Set yourself down and do an honest assessment. *Are you cocooning?* One way to know is by seeing what resonated with you in this chapter.

If you are, this activity can help you fly out.

If you haven't been spinning a cocoon, this is a great activity to keep you safe and protected without isolating yourself.

❖ *Design a mantle of protection.* I don't visualize so well, so I literally made myself a cloak. I got some felt and cut it into the shape of a full-length mantle.

Mine was small, about the size that would fit a big doll. I got shiny stars and spangles to adorn it. I sewed on a hood and cut out images of a jaguar and a buck and glued them on. I wrote the words I wanted on pieces of cloth and sewed them in as a lining. When I was done I pinned it onto a foam backing and hung it up.

❖ What would be best for you?

Draw one? Make one out of clay? Imagine one in your mind? Write a cloak song?

The options are unlimited, fully open to your imagination and your desire to stay in the world on your own terms -- safe, healthy and protected.

Here are some other ways to keep your isolation in check:

❖ Say yes to an invitation you might otherwise have neglected.

❖ Talk to a stranger – at a checkout counter, post office, video store, etc. Do it at least every second day.

❖ Make sure you are going out somewhere – movie, dinner, anywhere that's public at least once a week.

J is for Jerks

Zen Master Ryokan of Japan lived in a small hut at the bottom of a hill. He led a simple life. One night, a thief entered his hut but found nothing worth stealing. Upon Ryokan's return, he bumped right into the thief.

Ryokan said, "You might have come a long way, but I really do not have anything of value here. Yet, I cannot allow you to go back empty-handed.

The only thing I have that is of value here is the shirt on my back. I will give it to you as a gift." The thief took the shirt and left.

The half-naked Ryokan sat down and whispered to himself, "I wish that I could give him this beautiful moon!"

Hsing Yun's Ch'an Talk
www.buddhistdoor.com/OldWeb/bdoor/archive/zen_story/zen38.htm

There really are jerks out there and it seems natural to find some of them in our faces in the midst of Big Troubles. In kinder moments I think of them as people who lead unconscious lives.

But this book isn't about kinder moments or simpler times. It is about dealing with challenges, and those can include jerks. It is also about facing up to parts in ourselves that are misinformed about how we can best handle perceived insults, attacks and losses.

It is common to carry around a sense of impending doom when we are already feeling dumped on. "When it rains, it pours." "Bad things come in three's." "They'll kick you when you're down." These are but a few of the clichés directed at feeling like a tin can being mindlessly kicked down the block by an uncaring world.

That thinking is an ideal breeding ground for the most debilitating of emotions -- self-pity. It is the stuff of anger, fear, and frustration. Sooner or later it will lead to the question: "Why (poor) me?"

Anyone who has asked it knows it is not a helpful question. What is the best course of action right now would make a lot more sense. But we will have our moments, and our days. It's to be expected.

So what to do when your Very Bad Mood collides with some jerk's inappropriate, even obnoxious behavior?

Options:

Possibility #1: *Fly off the handle*. We probably will if we're either seriously over the edge or just letting our mouth move before our brain kicks in.

This is the easiest as well as the most detrimental to our well-being. It can strengthen fear's grip and weaken that of our better instincts.

Possibility #2: *Get on with your day*. Ignore it. Shake your head and go back to your life knowing you have bigger fish to fry than whatever that jerk hit on.

Possibility # 3: *Go one better.* Remember how you would have handled it when life was at its best and it was a Really *Good* Day. Take it up a notch, in a good way. Smile, offer a random act of kindness. Surprise them with compassion... Find Ryokan's moon and want to offer it to them.

There is another version of that Zen tale in which the thief is instantly enlightened and throws himself at the master's feet begging forgiveness. Over time he becomes Ryokan's most devoted pupil.

And no, I don't expect you'll gather a devoted following by taking the high road. On the other hand, who knows? We don't normally get to know the fallout from an unexpected act of kindness.

OK, forget the following. There are still big rewards for us if we can avoid being hurled into a negative spiral by some jerk, remembering that this is about us not them, this is our story, not their story.

Driving on the high road

Driving a car in Europe can make sitting in a New York taxi feel like a spa day. Austria, where I lived for some years, actually has speed limits but you wouldn't know it.

Sometimes a fast car would come up behind me out of nowhere. Suddenly I'd find the driver from hell an inch from my bumper, lights flashing, horn honking. For a while my reaction was to want to fight by slamming on the brake. That would annoy the hell out of them. Oh yeah. One day I had an 'aha' moment.

Only a jerk forgets that at 90 mph they are aiming a lethal weapon, not steering a car. I could choose to play a deadly game of chicken with a jerk or I could get out of the way.

Once I got my ego out of the driver's seat I would just signal and move over as soon as it was safe. Over time I noticed the same driver would climb up the next car's bumper. Jerk.

Giving in and moving into the 'jerk' world, we relinquish a fabulous opportunity to learn creative ways to cope. I found a lot on the other side of my aha moment. Like safety, pride, even exhilaration. By choosing the high road I freed myself from my own inner jerk and knee jerk reaction.

SAT's

If we were to consider coping with our current crisis something like taking the college boards, the SAT, then dealing with a jerk is the equivalent of taking a sample SAT.

Having someone in our face is a gift that can help us develop skills we need for coping with the Biggie. Yippee! We get to practice. We can fail and it's okay.

If we keep at it we will get better. If we get good enough, we'll have all the tools we need when the big days come our way.

Jerkativities

❖ Go to your naturscape. Recall a pet peeve of yours and your reactions. Now imagine dealing with it differently than you're used to; make it a stretch for you.

Find a way that you are proud of. Feel it vividly until you are comfortable with it. Take it back with you.

❖ Pick one part of your regular routine and find a small way to improve it. It doesn't matter what it is — it could be a smile to a barista, a compliment to a co-worker, or an offer to help a stranger. Be a little kinder than needed. The important part is to notice what you're doing and how it makes you feel.

❖ At least not directly. Remember the last person who annoyed you, the last jerk-infested situation you were in. *Note: this is designed to help with the small stuff; not the Big One.*

Check your physiology. Now imagine it again but keep smiling the whole time as you go through the scene in detail. If you feel negative emotions or feel your adrenaline kick in, make your smile bigger.

Keep at it until there is no more heat left. Now notice your physiology. Make a pact with your-self to remember how much better it feels when you smile.

is for Kicks

"The word 'silly' derives from the Greek 'selig' meaning 'blessed.' There is something sacred in being able to be silly."
Paul Pearsall in The Heart's Code. (Best-selling American author and speaker 1942-2007)

These are not kicks to jerks. These kicks go with giggles. Taking care of business during a rough patch is critical. We can't put our heads in the sand and hope tomorrow will be different.

There's a lot of hard work, self-discipline and stress in creating the changes we need to get us through a crisis and come out the better for it. *And* there is a time to pull down the curtain, sign off, drop out, and go for kicks and giggles.

One of the snares of a long-term crisis, be it health, legal, financial, relationship or other, is to think we're getting things done because we stay busy.

Quality busy

If we're coping with crisis we are not about to ignore its impacts. More likely we will obsess and overthink our stuff. Often we are not the best judge of how well we are doing. Sometimes we need reality checks, and sometimes we need a time out.

Ignoring this word to the wise has the inevitable result that awake or asleep we are still working, the life-as-art poster for unsustainability.

Periodically we all need to S T O P! Get away from self-inflicted routines. Bring a fresh perspective to our behavior. Recharge our batteries. Bring our life back into a healthier balance.

It isn't busy that fixes challenges and mends souls. It's good quality busy, and that requires discernment.

Letting go

Letting go is a challenge for managerial types. Allison described herself as one. She was mid-career as a bank manager, had two young children, an active lifestyle, and a husband who filed for divorce one day in September because he umm... 'met someone else.'

Allison was so busy managing the innumerable loose ends of her new life that she looked at me like I was a computer program that just crashed as I told her she needed to let go.

Allison equated safety with control, but took no time away from her challenges to gain the discernment she needed. She was too afraid her issues would eat her for lunch if she didn't keep stabbing away at them. Sadly the opposite was true. It took a physical breakdown for her to accept that her center would unravel long before anything in her outer world.

Allison created systems and activities that helped her feel in control. As she proudly told me early on: "I never met an issue I couldn't micro-manage." She prided herself on being able to hang on, even if by a thin strand. Her corporate life rewarded that behavior, and Allison was skillful at it.

Wending her way through a lengthy crisis offered no such benefits. Her 'A' personality tool kit offered little guidance for coming out of her crisis healthy, balanced and energized.

Sometimes her managerial skills did help her organize a busy life. The trick was learning when to stop, let go and allow herself to drift.

Stop kicking to find the kicks

Granted Allison's life was complicated and very busy. She believed firmly that her work and her children required her to ignore her own emotional turmoil. Granted it can be tempting, but it doesn't work that way.

Exactly in the midst of complexity we cannot ignore the inner workings of what makes us tick. Focusing exclusively on outer challenges without tending to our inner core may help us cope in the short run, but it cannot help us heal.

One way Allison slowly created more discernment was by taking time off for kicks and giggles. At first she resisted any schedule changes so we sought ways to help her replenish and relax that took no extra time.

Some days Allison took part of her lunch break to sit in a nearby park. Sometimes at lunch she sat in her car and sang, meditated, or journaled. Other times she just sat and breathed. A few nights a week she took a hot bath and drank a relaxing tea before going to sleep.

As the months passed Allison found ways to incorporate 'free' time into a packed schedule. I offered suggestions from my experience – getting to water, time in a garden, eating chocolate, a drive out of town with the kids.

Her issues and her kicks were not mine and that's just how it is. Yours are your own as well. Part of the value in making the effort to find k's & g's in crisis is that we get to know ourselves a bit better.

No sense acting like a trip to the local hangout will make you feel better just because it helps your best friend. We each need to find our own. It's part of getting the yin and yang, the warp and weave, the ups and downs of our own behavior.

Getting away for kicks and giggles won't change a damn thing about The Crisis. It won't make it better, and it also won't make it worse.

What it *will* do is reinvigorate our ability to cope.

Being pregnant in a good way

If a pregnant woman has sufficient vitamins and minerals, her fetus will take its nutrients from what is left over once her body's needs are met. If mom doesn't take care of herself the fetus will still get its nutrients, but it will come from her bone and her marrow and her essence.

A Big Crisis is just as uncompromising.

That's why like the pregnant woman who nurtures herself properly, sometimes we need to get away from our lives, get in our supply of kicks and giggles, and rev up to face the new morning. It will give us back the vital nutrients we have been using and replenish our severely tested coping quotient.

Your kicks and your giggles wait silently. They don't leap out from inside demanding play time. You have to go out of your way to catch them and take a recess. Okay, so it takes a little focus, you know there are worse things to focus on.

Kickativities

❖ What makes you happy?

This may seem like a no-brainer at first blush, but in the midst of ongoing challenges it may not be that simple after all.

Once you are clear, consider those as the most obvious opportunities for kicks & giggles.

P.S. The answer cannot be what you don't have. It has to be found within your current world of possibilities.

❖ Commit to a bit of indulgence. Incorporate it into your week. And your weekend.

❖ Incorporate one bit of indulgence into your daily routine.

❖ Sometimes it's hard to find a way to luxuriate. You can still have your kicks. You can always go back to the naturscape of your inner world and play in the safety of your imagination.

L is for Loss

"Give sorrow words. The grief that does not speak whispers o'er the -fraught heart, and bids it break."
William Shakespeare, (1564-1616)

Loss becomes part of our lives as we cope daily with crisis. I am not going to suggest that you should not care about your losses; I'm not that enlightened. Nor will I say loss is a part of life so get over yourself; I'm not that tough.

If you're in the midst of ongoing challenges not only are there ongoing losses to cope with. Most likely, some loss precipitated the crisis in the first place.

Choose carefully when you count

I have a lot to say about loss, but little that I can put out as advice. This is the exception:

Accept your losses, but don't count them. Reserve counting for what you have.

If you have losses to mourn - you have blessings to count and comfort lies in finding those and turning your spotlight on them.

If things are really tough, blessings may be pretty much all you have. If that sounds like a koan it's not meant as one.

There are sudden losses, such as receiving a cancer diagnosis, loss of a loved one, or losing a job. Then there are slower losses, often the result of an initial hit.

After a serious health diagnosis we have physical and emotional losses to cope with. The loss of a loved one may result in losing one's home, social life or way of life. A job loss may result in downsizing, relocation, loss of savings.

We are used to shunning serious illness and death, and similarly "nobody knows you when you're down and out." Most of us who have met with serious losses have been ignored by people who couldn't cope.

Even close friends and family are often unprepared and unable to support those of us coping with crisis and loss.

Any of these can send us into a tailspin. No two people experience loss the same; and no two people grieve their losses the same.

On loss and gaining

By now many of us are familiar with Elisabeth Kubler-Ross's work on death, dying and loss. She identified five stages in terminally ill patients: denial, anger, depression, bargaining, and acceptance.

Her greatest contribution was not to provide stages of grief, but to legitimize grief and bring it into public awareness.

Open acceptance of grief offers an indelible support. Encouragement to proceed with grieving and coping as we see fit is a precondition to healing.

Loss and grief are described in steps, but that's a little misleading. The stages of grief were never intended as a step ladder. Most of us are likely to cycle back and forth within the stages as we cope with loss. Some of us may cope well by going through only some of these steps.

The ways are as individual as we are, but the goals are the same:

- ✓ Find ways to accept our new lives

- ✓ Acknowledge small losses while grieving deeply for larger ones

- ✓ Make sure we know the difference

- ✓ Re-engage in life, hope, and dreams.

You have probably already noticed that hiding from pain doesn't make it go away. That includes hiding in legal and illegal drugs.

Reaching out to the other side

I already gave you the only advice I had on loss. Now I will share with you what has helped me. Perhaps you have tried some already. If they don't hold any appeal, you could consider similar supports that have meaning for you.

Calming natural remedies. These have been via many modalities and have helped in many ways. They include herbs, Bach Flowers, hypnotherapy, acupuncture, massage, Reiki and many other forms of energy work.

Deepening my connections with the natural world. This has happened at many levels and in many ways. Journeys to wild places, gardening, walks, sitting and looking, talking to trees and plants, writing in and about nature...

Animal comforts. This includes petting, walking and being loved by my dogs, relating well to a few stuffed animals. Hugging them. Getting backyard chickens and spending time watching them, enjoying their eggs. Feeding them. Appreciating little bugs. Even snakes.

Journaling. I journaled in fits and starts, and it was always enormously helpful. I think I have volumes.

Speaking Truth. I gave up pretending to be tough. I emoted and cried when I needed, named my feelings and emotions, and here and there indulged in all-out self-pity.

Body care. I took classes and on my own practiced a martial art, yoga and worked out. Rowing gave me the feeling of moving forward and was a gym favorite. Sometimes it was really hard to get going, and sometimes all I could do was take a walk. It was *always* worth it.

Relationships. I have a partner, and keeping that relationship solid, emotionally and physically was a salve for my wounds. If you live alone, I would recommend scheduling regular quality friend time. Intimacy and community are great assets in the coping tool box.

Reaching out to help others. This includes talking to people who I knew were suffering but I might have previously ignored. Writing this book helped me reach out. Offering up prayers to those in need. Volunteering.

Dreaming. See **D is for Dreams**. Absolutely essential. Pretty much most of the letters in this ABC book are about tools and techniques that have helped me.

Gratitude. See **G is for Gratitude**. It is the best antidote I know to feelings of loss.

Smiles. Smiles given, smiles accepted, smiles of all kind helped. I went through a period where each morning the moment I awoke my chest tightened and my stomach tensed.

So I decided as soon as my eyes were open to breathe deeply and put a smile on my face.

The losses, the damage, the crises I faced were still the same. But my face as I confronted them changed.

Lossativities

❖ As you cope with your Big Crisis, how are you dealing with the losses?

❖ If you are using any of the tools and techniques that helped me, which do you rely on the most?

❖ If you are not and you had to pick two, which would they be?

❖ How do you feel about this? *"Accept your losses, but don't count them. Reserve counting only for what you have."*

Consider sharing your response with someone who understands your situation.

m is for Mind

"Above all, watch with glittering eyes the whole world around you because the greatest secrets are always hidden in the most unlikely places. Those who don't believe in magic will never find it." **Roald Dahl**, (British writer of children's stories 1916 – 1990)

Our minds are nowhere near as important as they would have us believe. Yes our brains are huge. Our brain encompasses or is linked to our entire being, including that one noisy, often annoying layer we think of as our mind.

That layer is our conscious awareness, and it's really not able to do all that much without input from regions of our brain we tend to ignore. Those unexplored, subconscious areas of mind are formative. Ignored or not, they are formidable in their overarching reach in shaping our lives. Knowing the components of the subconscious mind explains why.

Do you mind?

Our *emotions* are enormously powerful. Our *instincts* drive us. Our *myths* determine our beliefs and define our outer boundaries. Our *prayers* and *dreams* are a huge part of our psyche and open up great opportunities for change.

Science and social theorists agree that these essential drivers do not reside in the narrow upper echelons of mind.

Beyond that fundamental agreement debates rage on the specifics of mind-body-spirit interactions. I'm not attempting to join the philosophers, sociologists and neurologists in running debates that are beyond my ken. They can work on what, why and wherefore. I'm only interested in the *how* of change.

I want to offer you practical applications. Essential to this pragmatic framework is an understanding how we can use the more unfamiliar parts of our mind to control our thoughts, emotions and life energies. Once we know who is in charge we have access to how we are living our lives. Reaching the prime movers of change holds the key to self-determination.

If handed a Big One our rational mind immediately starts asking questions. The best answers are found by understanding what drives us, recognizing our coping skills, finding happiness no matter what, and learning to change beliefs that no longer serve us well.

Somewhere under the prism...

For the sake of conversation, let's put aside a conscious Minds-R-Us paradigm. Let's replace it with a prism based on access to deeper regions. Most of us have a natural affinity to prisms. Who doesn't like a rainbow?

How totally cool is it to shoot a narrow light beam through a prism and watch it come out broader than when it entered and shiny it its rainbow colors.

Now imagine placing a prism between your conscious thinking and your less accessible areas of mind. What comes out on the other side will be vaster, deeper, and more colorful than what went in.

Once we know how to pass through that prism at will, a rainbow world of opportunity and change awaits.

There we are free to change our inner monologue, brighten and expand our dreams, change repetitive emotional responses, and ultimately create a world of our choosing.

As a hypnotherapist, my first task with clients is to explain the role of the mind in goal-setting and change. Most people are familiar with Las Vegas shows where people on stage cluck like chickens or Hollywood movies where a hypnotist uses mind control to bend a person to his will.

Understandably many clients are fearful of hypnosis. As familiar as these clichés are, few people know that the hypnotic trance state is one we are in and out of several times a day – all on our own.

Most people considering hypnotherapy have no idea how easy it is to dive through their own prisms and connect with their subconscious mind.

Even more important, they are entirely unaware of the massive changes even one such targeted experience can make.

Yakity-yak will hold you back

Our conscious mind is extremely active. It's great at rational problem-solving, puzzles, debates, analysis, and rationalization. It's great for short-term recall and Monday morning quarterbacking. It's also a chatter-box.

It yaks at us non-stop. It can wear us down with its incessant demands, criticisms and nervous chatter. Although 90% of our thoughts are repetitive we listen to them day in, day out.

We can easily end up living endless loops that are dominated by what Taoists labeled "monkey mind."

"She shouldn't wear skirts like that, her calves are so ugly." "Why did my boss look at me that way?" "I'm too x,y,z…" "I'm not good, big, pretty, strong, tough enough…" Well for that matter, neither is he, she, it, and so on and so forth.

This is terrible enough when life is good. But when we're dealing with Heavy Stuff, we can drown in these negative spirals.

Controlling monkey mind

The conscious mind is the analytical part of our brain. The unconscious mind and autonomic nervous system control functions that keep us alive like breathing lungs and a beating heart.

In between the two our subconscious mind delineates the boundaries of *how* we lead the lives we have been given.

Even though it acts like head honcho, our self-talking conscious mind works within a command and control system in which it has no control and where the commands are dictated by the subconscious mind.

Old monkey mind that thinks it's the be-all and end-all is really nothing more than a lackey. It can do neither more nor less than exactly what it is told. If we are ready to make changes that's actually good news!

Even one intentional trip through our own prism has the potential to change information we have stored at command central since childhood.

Given the right input, our subconscious mind will take us from that dark night to the sunny days. What had been grounds for Anxiety easily transmutes into Zowie!

Once it gets new input, our subconscious mind will be exactly as repetitive, powerful, dogged and dictatorial about its new understanding as it had been about our age-old outdated beliefs.

The entire process can be easier and much faster than you may imagine. It can also be a lot of fun. In any case it opens a dialogue with the part that has most likely been trying to get you to listen in for a long time.

I think that's really good news. We can change and we can change NOW. Check out **N**, because **N is for Now**.

Mindativities:

❖ Today listen in to your mental chatter. Plan on listening in at least five times during the day.

What do you hear? Check for patterns. Listen in for what is repeated.

Is there any information or commentary you don't want to keep hearing?

Find one, and make note of it. Then make time for intentional change.

❖ Remember the first exercise under **A**? Go to your safe haven. When you are feeling comfortable, put out a question relating to the chatter – for example, where did I learn that I wasn't good enough? Or that I wasn't successful? Or that I had to keep putting myself down?

Allow an answer to be shown to you, to hear it, or sense it. Return that belief to its rightful owner and replace it with your highest and best intention for yourself.

Know that in the most challenging of times you have started to become who you want to be in life's finest moments.

Smile and gently return.

n is for Now

"Somewhere over the rainbow bluebirds fly. Birds fly over the rainbow. Why then oh why can't I?"
Harold Arlen, music **and Yip Harburg,** lyrics

Especially in times of crisis we tend to revert to the known, and that doesn't only mean comfort food. It's also old habits and thoughts, old ways of viewing the world, and familiar ways of functioning. Fact is, it may have been some of those old patterns that helped bring the crisis on us. See **B is for Beliefs.**

If we accept that there are deep subconscious habits and beliefs that govern our perceptions and reactions, we must also acknowledge the power of the ones we may not like, but still have.

So how do we change?

In **M is for Mind** we looked at the command-control system of the subconscious. Now let's look specifically at how to change. We can start with this:

Let's jump in.

Let's jump in NOW!

Any difference in those two? Remember as a child when mom would say something like "Come on, we have to go," and you would continue to play. Mom might ask again and get the same result. She might explain why you need to go, or tempt you with TV or cookies. And you might still prefer to play. But mom invariably gets your attention when she says "That's it. We have to go -- NOW."

Those Mom and Dad finger-pointing, hands-on-hips NOW's went straight into the deepest recesses of our minds and took up permanent residence. Our subconscious minds accepted them unflinchingly and with no equally strong challenge to them they will live there for a lifetime at least.

Some words hold more power over us than others. The simple three-letter command NOW holds enormous sway over our lives. To fully understand its power we need to go back to the subconscious mind and understand a little more of its workings.

How do we change NOW?

The common spiritual injunction is not 'Be Here,' but 'Be Here Now.' Similarly, Eckhart Tolle's "The Power of Now" is among the most influential of all modern spiritual books.

Now is a clarion call to our subconscious minds to obey instantly ("or else"). It's why the word *now* is lodged repetitively in most hypnotic commands.

How does this knowledge help us when life is one Big Fat Crisis Now? Obviously not everything can be instantly changed, nor does everything need to be. But often our attitude about what we are facing does need either support or change.

Often the reversal of fortune we so desperately seek demands an internal reframing of how we view our circumstances. All things change when we do. When we connect with our subconscious minds

...If we give it a clear task or goal, ...if we get its agreement, ...if we get it to accept the change NOW!

We made deep and permanent change. Period.

If this sounds too good to be true, it's not. I have helped hundreds of people to stop smoking in just one session. I used a second session for assurance, but the work got done in less than two hours. Sure I missed some, but no other stop smoking method approaches anything like the 85% success rate I had with smokers.

In other areas as well, as a hypnotherapist I have seen change that was so quick and so powerful it knocked my socks off.

It all gets down to the hypnotherapist's favorite trick question: Where do you live? Answer: In your mind.

If you walk away from this book applying nothing more than the following pointers, your life will improve and expand in utterly amazing ways. Guaranteed.

Critical pieces for working with our subconscious.

Accept that the process of change is what it is. It can be gentle, easy, or a wild ride. It may come in sounds, images, shapes, colors, sensations sighs or whispers.

It may come with tears or a whimper, with laughter or chills. There are as many different modes and responses as there are intentional connections to our subconscious minds.

Visualization became very popular in the 70's, but for many of us it failed in its promise of great change. For some it was the word itself – not everyone is primarily visual.

Get into the right state of Mind. Another problem with the New Age version of visualization was a lack of discernment. The repetitive yada yada self-talk chatter splatter brain wave activity precludes a connection to the deeper parts of mind.

During waking hours our minds function at the quick Beta brain wave level. There are exceptions for daydreaming, dancing, listening to music and other trancelike activities.

In Beta we can look in the mirror repeating a lifechanging phrase until we're old and gray with the only result that eventually we are old and gray. It is entirely different when we do exactly the same thing in the right state of awareness.

To connect with our deeper subconscious mind we need to be in the slower brain wave state called Alpha. There change may happen instantaneously.

Learn easy steps to connect with your subconscious. I'll go into some detail on how to do that when we come to the NOWativities.

Know what your subconscious mind needs. It is passive, so it needs your emotion. *No strong emotion = no change.*

It accepted its present belief partly through repetition, so *repetition* is also essential.

The subconscious mind is a huge container. It is not a thinking part of us in the way of our conscious mind. It holds old memories, belief systems, our flight or fight reflex.

It is literal; so don't joke around with your subconscious. It's simple-minded. Be crystal clear in your messages. It can't do fuzzy.

It needs a new task or approach to replace the one you're changing. This is critical. When we take one belief or function away we *must* replace it with another or the old ways *will* return.

It needs to agree. Think of talking with a kid, or negotiating change with someone. It is essential to answer all questions and work through to an agreed upon outcome.

Trust. Trust the process. This is not the time to question whether or not you're really, really in trance or in raise any other analytical doubts. That's a surefire track out the door and into the conscious mind.

Trust your deeper mind. One of the major functions of the subconscious mind is to protect you. It will *always* do its best for you. If what you're doing appears self-destructive, for example cigarette smoking, it's not because your subconscious mind is out to kill you.

It's because it misunderstood something and is laboring under the illusion that cigarettes are what you need. When it understands that is bad for you and you show it a new way, change is immediate.

Recognize that time is non-existent in the subconscious. In the deep recesses of our mind we don't know past or future. Only present, only the Here and Now. When we remember a trauma we don't recall it, we *relive* it. This is another reason NOW is so important.

If this seems like a lot, it's just because it's spelled out. It's actually a simple, almost formulaic process. We've got the formula. Now let's get to the practice.

NOWativities.

❖ Pick a belief or habit you truly want to change. Be really clear about it. Formulate it simply. Once you are clear about what you want and determined to get it, it is time to meet the boss. Here's how.

❖ Review the critical pieces again before you start this practice.

❖ Always choose a time when you will be undisturbed. Use a comfortable chair and wear comfortable clothing. Find a relaxed position.

By the way, your Naturscape is a wonderful place to do any of this work.

- ❖ To get to the subconscious we need to quiet the mental chatter and relax. The more we relax, the more quiet our mind becomes. The quieter it is, the more we relax. That's it.

- ❖ The subconscious mind is passive and can't tell the difference between something real and something *strongly, repeatedly and emotionally imagined.* Can't emphasize that enough.

- ❖ When you are fully relaxed, open the discussion. Now explain to the powerful subconscious mind easily exactly what you want to change and enlist its support.

- ❖ The subconscious mind appreciates emotion-filled, positive suggestions combined with powerful belief.

- ❖ If your thoughts start to wander gently bring yourself back and focus on the suggestions.

- ❖ Bring this to a conclusion using each critical piece.

- ❖ Gently, confidently, bring yourself back.

O is for Odd

"We have always found the Irish a bit odd. They refuse to be English." **Winston Churchill** (British orator, author and prime minister. 1874-1965)

Like I said in **J**, there are jerks out there. If they're in your life at all it will be on the wrong side of what's right for you.

During crisis, clients sometimes express deep shock at other people's behavior or unexpected reactions. Sometimes these were beyond their ability to categorize or understand.

Attempting to do so for them won't help, it would be my interpretation not theirs. And the problem is that before they can categorize or understand, say nothing of resolve, they have to move beyond the judgment-laden shock.

Frequently the description of the offending behavior, event or person is something like: "They are an expletive, expletive, expletive!!!" It's a way to release pain and gain a sense of separate-ness, but it doesn't help with understanding. Neither does it offer a sustained way of coping.

The truth is that absent some cord that connects us to an event, we hopelessly attempt to understand one unknown with another. We pretty much have to come up empty because like the proverbial Martian viewing human behavior, we are observing an alien world that speaks an unknown tongue.

Hung out to dry should be only for clothes

Janet told me she felt deserted by people for whom she would have 'put her hand in the fire.' She said she was 'stunned' by much of what happened at the personal level as she and her family maneuvered through lengthy legal and financial battles. Her feeling of living in an alien world was becoming debilitating.

Similarly, when Susan first confronted bankruptcy she described it as an 'unintelligible piece,' saying she had no internal programming to prepare her for it. Struggling to pay bills was known. So were occasional rough patches. But this, she said, was unlike anything she imagined could 'happen here.'

That dazzling sense of unreality left her disconnected an unable to cope with day to day decisions.

The core self we lean on for strength during times of crisis can feel attacked and we can feel like we have become bait for emotional vultures and people we once thought we knew or loved.

I describe this to my clients as feeling dangled above their own life like laundry on a clothes line. Only clothes should be hung out to dry. Nobody deserves to feel that isolated. We needed to explore ways to stop the dangling and start reconnecting.

Oddly enough, this helped.

Here's what I suggest for this sense of astonishment.

First I created a category and named it *odd*. Anything they couldn't accept or make emotional sense of I asked them to put into the category of odd.

Odd is what that Martian, once over the initial shock, might consider our eating habits. Odd is often accompanied by a head scratch or a wistful smirk. It might even elicit a grin.

That is exactly the felt sense I wanted them to get as the first step in moving beyond an incredulous sense of hurt, anger or shock.

Odd offers cover to anyone in crisis who is unhappy with how others react. It takes away some of the emotional bite. It is a great start, but we still need to come down off the clothes line. We need to land in territory that is at least somehow familiar, and we need to bring our wounded emotional self back home.

This is really important in a long-term crisis. Otherwise circumstance, confusion, jerks, mean people, new hits and more will take their bites.

We will be left beyond stunned. Our sense of self-worth can feel mangled and mostly devoured from the mean bites.

Changing the odds

Once we have ascribed *odd* to otherwise inexplicable behavior and events it is time to look at ourselves. We need to take inventory and assess how well we are handling our own issues.

Some we should treat like a toothache and get a professional to help us out. Some we should reframe as stepping stones and celebrate each small step.

Sometimes we may need to remind ourselves that we are in the shifting sands of change, and a minor quake can propel us forward.

Above all, we need to remember who we truly are. We also want to remind ourselves of who we want to be as we journey through our crisis, and who we want to become as we lay the foundation for sunny days ahead.

The wise one in the moment

If we are totally overwhelmed by a moment we can learn to change who we are in that moment.

We can learn to rely on our internal wise woman or wizard. We can temporarily shapeshift into the one who trusts that *no matter what* we will handle it.

This image has gotten me through some excruciatingly difficult moments such as waiting for test results or going into surgery. It did more than get me through. It let me be the person I wanted to become.

Even if we only do this for some moments, it is a great personal victory. It begins by moving the unintelligible into the category of *odd*, and then freeing ourselves of the attachments.

The oddativities below will help you find that freedom by moving into a state of detachment and personal empowerment. From there we can compassionately and safely let shift happen.

Oddativities

❖ Look back at a past crisis. It really needs to be one you are beyond. Recall when someone crossed a line with you and you went over the edge. There should still be some 'bite' connected to the memory.

Once you've found it allow yourself to indulge a little in some negative emotions or anxiety.

Once you feel some emotion, reframe the event as *odd*.

Each time you want to throw an emotionally-laden adjective at it, relabel it. Call it **ODD** until the sting is gone. Welcome to the wonderful world of *odd*!

❖ Find your naturscape. Experience an event in any way that brings up the bite and some negative emotions.

Get a (really) magic marker and paint a big **X** over that scene including the negative emotions you have surrounding that person or event.

Destroy that picture in whatever way comes to you. Burn it or cut it into little pieces, send it off into outer space... whatever.

Now replace it with an image of the desired outcome. Make sure you feel really good with the changed scene. Feel the positive emotions strongly.

Wrap that scene in pink or frame it in gold, whatever feels to you like you are immortalizing and honoring it.

Breathe it into your whole body. Feel it in your heart. Not only are you done, but you are done with that issue now, forever. Gently return.

P is for Physical

"Let's get physical, physical, I wanna get physical, let's get physical. Let me hear your body talk, your body talk, let me hear your body talk"... ("Physical"# 1 hit written by **Steve Kipner** 1981, recorded by **Olivia Newton-John** 1982)

Shall we? Until now we have considered the mind, psyche, and emotions, but we are undeniably physical. We may love our bodies or hate them, but we got them and they got us, babe.

Our bodies are our canaries in the coal mine, so listening in to our physical selves will tell us a great deal about the impact life is having on us. But we need to listen, and sometimes we don't want to, sometimes we don't know how.

What's a life without a body?

In crisis we may just chalk up any surprise health issues to more collateral damage. We may tell ourselves we'll deal with it another time, when life is better.

Or we may be in good health now and dealing with our physical selves gets placed on the lowest step of the huge to-do ladder. Here is the fallacy in that thinking:

When we are in crisis our bodies yearn for TLC. This is not me being touchy-feely; this is human physiology.

91

Our bodies react to anxiety, stress and depression in ways that will tend to perpetuate anxiety, stress and depression.

Blame the endocrine system. If we live with ongoing stresses, our endocrine system supports us by working our adrenals hard so they produce the adrenaline it believes we need for survival.

Once triggered, the fight/flight mechanism primes us for a life-death battle. Our system will not make the fine distinction between a physical threat to our life and a threat to life as it once was. Its job is to ready us for the kill and it *will* do its job.

Adrenaline kicks in hard and fast and releases only slowly. In a Big Crisis we face many anxiety-producing moments with the result that physiologically we can end up living in adrenal overdrive. Over time this can wreak havoc on our bodies!

This is one reason we must seek ways to protect ourselves at all levels, mental, emotional, spiritual and physical. We can prevent stress-related damage, especially if we are listening in before symptoms appear. A symptom is our body's way of pounding on our door since we ignored the gentle taps. It lets us know things are likely to get worse if we don't change course.

For better and sometimes for worse, our bodies are amazingly compliant. The accommodating way that our bodies respond to thirst is a simple and powerful example of this mechanism.

If we consistently ignore our thirst signals, rather than screaming at us 'you're thirsty you idiot. Go get water now!' it goes the other way and stops telling us we are thirsty. This makes it easy for us to continue.

With thirst, fatigue and dark urine are early warning signals. If we ignore those, we can develop an electrolyte imbalance with its host of attendant issues. If we ignore that, well no need to be morbid; you get the trajectory.

The opposite is also true. A glass of water is worth a great deal more than may be apparent. Our body is just as accommodating, but in a way that benefits us.

If we listen in and drink water when we are thirsty we maintain a good energy level and support our natural inclination toward health and balance. The key phrase is listening in.

That's how we get physical! In crisis this is all magnified. We get extra credit for taking special care of our bodies. It won't stop the crisis, but with our body on our side we have a powerful ally to help us meet those challenges.

Our immune system, nervous system, and brain cells, all work better when we need them most. We will feel more complete, more aware and more capable. We get the good stuff flowing and keep the bad at bay. That should be worth a little extra effort, n'est ce pas?

Yet exactly when we need it most is when we are likely to hear our inner Eeyore telling us it doesn't matter anyway, why bother, life is in the crapper, etc. etc. When Eeyore kicks in it's time to shut that noise down and find something soothing and nurturing.

That's when you move – even a little. Sometimes talking, even to ourselves, just won't do it. Sometimes it's just time to get in motion – to get physical!

During a Big One, life improves amazingly just by incorporating into our lives as much of this as possible:

- ✓ Eat well, sleep well and drink well.

- ✓ Find what nurtures you and incorporate it into your life.

- ✓ Touch and be touched.

- ✓ Smile and be smiled at.

- ✓ MOVE!

- ✓ Listen in to know what you need when you need it.

- ✓ Be honest with yourself.

In short, you need to become your own stoplight and recognize your colors: **Stop** *on red,* **Rest** *on orange, and* **Go** *like hell on green!*

Physativities

❖ Listen in right now. Thirsty? Tired? Bored? Exasperated? What, if anything, would you like to do about it? Go ahead, just do it.

❖ If you have a pet, consider spending more time together. We humans get a lot of nurturing when a living being is happy to see us.

❖ If your situation doesn't allow for a pet consider a plant, a stuffed animal or a pet tree.

❖ Find some way to add movement into your life. It can be anything – from parking further away in a mall lot or bending more as you clean, to adding a few minutes to your workout, adding a physical activity to your weekend...

❖ Keep in mind how important it is to move and wherever you see the opportunity, dance, sing, play, walk... just Get Physical.

@ is for Questions

"Good questions outrank easy answers." **Anonymous**

So many questions; so few answers. That keeps coming up as a constant for people coping with Big Ones. Distinguishing types of questions can help break some old ruts. Three types of questions are sure to be there:

Questions that come at you from others. There are times when even simple "Hey, what's up? Or "How have you been?" can give you pause.

Questions you need to ask of others. Information that is important to you.

Finally, questions you ask yourself, sometimes repetitively, sometimes at 4 a.m., or in the middle of something entirely unrelated.

Questions from others

In some ways these are easiest to deal with since they're not so likely to haunt you in the middle of the night. In other ways these can be deceptively simple because they may touch on piles of stuff underlying not only your answers, but the questions themselves.

When it comes to questions, two big issues impact how you answer.

First who's asking? Really. Is the person your friend, foe, colleague, former colleague, drama queen (or king), town gossip, trusted family member, or someone else. The list of possibilities is long with many shades of closeness, trust, and hidden agendas.

My advice is this: Whatever you decide to say or not say, *do not lie*. Not even a teensy fib. Not even on your worst days.

If a clerk asks "And how are you today?" and you feel like death warmed over, parry with something like: "Hey, how about yourself?" or "It's hot out today. Trying to stay cool."

You may want to thrust with "I'm sucky, my life is in bits and pieces and it's none of your damn business, so back off!" That might work except for my other bit of advice.

Imagine what you say might end up on the front page of the newspaper. Not that it's likely, but thinking it is a good way to be cautious about what you say. You are already battling on enough fronts, you don't need any more issues.

The second part of answering others is who you are as you journey through your crisis. Are you a role model for others? Are you writing blogs and columns to the newspaper about what the experience is like? Are you sharing your situation only with trusted friends and family? Are you somehow in hiding?

All of these will influence what you say, how loud and how often you say it, and to whom. A new 'friend' that came to you through your difficulties may be comforting now, but they have not withstood the test of time. They may just love the drama of it all. Use discretion and your best judgment.

Questions to others

The second kind of question is what you should ask of others. If you got laid off, for example, you knew to ask about unemployment.

But there may be a lot more support out there than you know. The level of crisis right now is societal, with massive economic fallout. Layoffs are but one of the many direct and indirect aspects of crisis.

A positive result is the increase in the range of support opportunities. There are many more arenas from which you can seek help than ever before.

Different types of professionals are helping pro bono. Neighborhood outreach, community information resources, and support groups have formed. So have Internet chat groups and information resources.

It's a pretty good bet that you are not alone in what you seek. Do your homework. Make use of available resources and opportunities.

Go the extra mile

Research your situation. Reach beyond your regular monologues and dialogues and networks. Stretch.

You may find alternatives and opportunities you never dreamed of. You may have a support network waiting to help guide you over the hump. Maybe not, but you won't know unless you check it out.

Do battle with any voices that tell you you're alone, that it was your fault or say that if only you had or hadn't done this, that, or the other it would have been different.

These are guilty sounds that rise to the surface in crisis. They're wrong and they need to be answered or they will keep coming back and sap your strength.

You can handle those negative voices as you do people. Some you may want to acknowledge and move on. If it seems like it may be fruitful, answer the voices.

You can also tell yourself those voices may be right on the mark a*nd it doesn't matter.* All that matters now is finding a way through. That should soften up the inside noise enough so you can proactively do some problem-solving.

It's 4 in the morning...

Finally there are questions that rattle around and around and around. Answer them if you have an answer that will stop the repetitive questioning.

You could also try ignoring them. I really don't recommend it though. They are more likely to come back harder and stronger. There is a third way. You can postpone them.

Later for you!

This is a great middle of the night technique. It acknowledges the question. You can even express gratitude to the question. Then indicate it's way too important to answer during the night. Roll over and go back to sleep.

Searching for answers in that state is a good formula for sinking into an abyss of worry and unanswered 'what if's.' Give yourself a break. Accept that you are tired, you are in crisis, it's the middle of the night and your judgment is impaired.

An insidious impact of crisis is not even realizing when our judgment is impaired.

Or 4 in the afternoon...

Most clients understand the value of turning off the trouble switch at 4 a.m. But what about 4 p.m.? During the day when questions give no peace another approach is called for.

This is a technique I call kill it with kindness. Acknowledge the terrible worries, the importance of the question. Then embellish. Take it all the way into a worst case scenario. That scenario is the reason the question is repetitive anyway, so go for it. But be prepared. Ask that questioning part of mind "And then?" relying on the technique presented in **F is for Frantic**.

Once you are out of answers to 'and then,' you have nailed the real question – and the real fear. Acknowledge its importance and resolve that it is in fact too important to answer now.

Tell yourself you will answer it when you can take more time, or after you have talked to someone, or once something else happens, or if Plan B fails.

Don't leave it hanging; give it something to look forward to, and close the discussion. This process is a simple way to gain a great deal of peace of mind.

Should you decide to tackle the question make absolutely sure you are up to the task of providing an answer that is acceptable to your rational mind and honest at deeper levels.

Be a good friend to yourself. Don't even try if it's 4 a.m., if you've just had an argument, you're weepy, depressed or rushed.

Learn to give it a rest and let yourself be.

Here's the Q & A in brief:

- ✓ When asked a question be honest, no matter how much or how little you choose to reveal. Think headlines.

- ✓ If you have questions about your situation, be creative, resolute, persistent, and seek help.

- ✓ If unproductive questions keep at you repetitively, be compassionate with yourself. They too shall pass. Keep practicing your coping skills.

Questativities

- ❖ Do you have a clear perspective as to how open you want to be about your situation?

  There is comfort in consistency.

- ❖ If you are not open about your situation, are you checking to make sure you are not in a shaming and blaming mode?

- ❖ What avenues of support and help do you have? Are you sure you have explored all avenues and are maximizing available resources?

- ❖ Review how to deal with your own questions and be nice. To yourself.

R is for Remember

"...Deep in December, it's nice to remember, without a hurt the heart is hollow. Deep in December, it's nice to remember, the fire of September that made us mellow. Deep in December, our hearts should remember And follow." Words by lyricist **Tom Jones**, *('Try to Remember'* is a song from *The Fantasticks.*)

There is a flow of learning, forgetting and remembering that continues throughout our lives. I say now is the time for remembering, but not everything. Only the good stuff, the important stuff.

I have learned acupressure massage, acupoint massage, self-massage, reflexology and muscle testing and more. There's a list of relaxation techniques that would easily fill a page and certainly bore you to tears.

The same holds for meditation methods. As a trained hypnotherapist and as an herbalist I have other amazing self-help skills.

*But if I knew only one style of breath control or but one way to relax that would be enough -- if **I remember to use it**.*

I have had days I was so tense I could barely move my neck, my lower back caused me pain when I walked, and my head felt like it would burst. I have had days filled with anxiety and tears, depression and stomach aches.

Did I rely on my basket of skills? Well, honestly yes, sometimes. In the beginning it was almost an afterthought, like if I happened to remember. Later that turned into consciously seeking to remember.

Ultimately, after remembering over and over what I kept forgetting, I no longer had to remember. I couldn't forget the skills if I tried.

What's with that forgetting our special skills anyway? It's very common; in fact it happens to all of us sometimes, even those of us who teach this stuff.

Rhetorical question, but I learned to remember, and the good news is this: As the neurotic detective Mr. Monk said to Sharona about overcoming her fear of elephants: "If I can do it, anyone can."

So what do we really need to remember?

Top five things to remember to remember:

First and most important: Whatever you are going through will end. Change is inevitable and you will be there to witness it.

Second: You have coping skills. From knowing how to cross a busy street in traffic to unraveling the mysteries of human interactions, you have already learned more than you know.

Third: Whatever it is, *you* are bigger than *it*. While it may throw you off your game for a time, you know how to pick yourself up and dust yourself off. You've done it before and even if this one is bigger and lasts longer, the principles are the same.

Fourth: Reframing is reclaiming. Before Janet's protracted crisis she had spent a lot of money on her washer and dryer. They were top of the line and as eco-friendly as she could find. They were a symbol of the care she took of her family's needs.

She became obsessed with losing them. She described them as a supporting beam and how their loss would mean the roof could collapse any moment.

Together we reframed. We turned them into a symbol of the ignorance and difficulties that were closing in on her and her family. Losing them would free her from some of the values that held her trapped.

As the financial burdens increased she decided to sell them. We continued reframing. Rather than 'losing' them she was choosing to sell them. She would find them a good home and we get good money in exchange.

It was a simple readjustment, but it changed the frame and empowered her enormously. She transformed a symbol of pain and fear into self-determination and a ticket to freedom.

Fifth: You know what you need. Make time for it, even if you don't think you can or should or don't believe you've earned it. If nothing else, go back over the good stuff in these chapters that you want to remember, and go with those.

How to remember to remember

The five majors may seem to beg the question of how to remember in the midst of a raging storm. How do we remember to rest, love, smile, keep focus and reframe as needed?

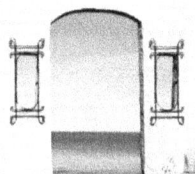

I only know one way that works for sure, and that's *coming back to the quiet center inside*: Returning, over and over, again and again, until it becomes a part of where we live.

In each of us there is a place that is hopeful and curious, ageless, timeless and fully safe. It's shapeless until we give it form. It's like a duffel bag filled with goodies.

We go there and open our gifts, over and over. As we do that they fill again. Endless presents in an timeless presence.

It is a place of yearning – for connection to the 'unbearable lightness of being,' to the roots and rays of life, to unlimited being. It is out of place, time, and outside human drama.

What we need to remember is that it is accessible.

When we touch that place, at least for a moment we have everything we could ever need to succeed.

We can glide there on the breath, we can find it in our naturscape, or in the moments before or after sleep.

We can find it in a tree or as we count ourselves into prayer. We can get there through song or dance, through a chant or a pose, through total stillness or a scent in the wind.

The ways into timelessness are scattered throughout this book.

We remember to remember by slowly slowing down enough so we can come to a full stop.

When we stop fully and are still inside, time stops with us. There is only the moment and the storms do not exist.

Then, in that state of graced presence, when we reach into our duffel bag of presents we have the certainty that we will indeed find exactly the right coping tool, and our needs will be met.

Remembativities:

❖ What would you like to reframe? Find it, play devil's advocate with it. Change it. Expand it. Hold the new frame until it feels familiar.

❖ Put down the book, close your eyes and hum to yourself. Rock a little. Sway like a tree in the breeze. If you have a question, allow an answer to find you. If you have no question, dip into the well and find refreshment.

❖ Identify a coping skill that once helped you get over a broken heart, a financial loss or a physical problem. Hold it in your mind's eye. Take the skill and turn it into a shield, a coat of arms or a cloak.

❖ Decorate it. Fondle it. Put it on. Honor it. Make it your own. Allow yourself to emote; feel it in you, on you, around you. Rub your thumb and index finger together as you feel it intensely.

❖ Later in the same day, remember. Rub your fingers together and let the same feelings well up. The more you do this the stronger it gets. Feel the protection, the power, the love. It is one of your tools and fully accessible.

You need only remember.

S is for Stones

"Life throws stones at you, but your love and your dream change those stones into the flowers of discovery. ...People like you enrich the dreams of the world, and it is dreams that create history." **Ben Okri** (an award-winning Nigerian author b. 1959)

I like stones. I think we too easily overlook the importance of stones in our lives. They are deeply embedded in the human psyche in so many ways.

We who have moved from caves of stone to homes of stone speak of stepping stones along our paths.

We have engraved them, painted them, turned them into runes, used them as divination and decoration, as wheels, to sharpen instruments; we create beautiful pottery, magnificent statues and works of art.

We use them in our most enduring and magnificent monuments, in our mysterious pyramids and at places of worship like Stonehenge.

We skip them over water for the sheer joy of it. We have long used them in our sau- saunas and sweat lodges and for relaxing massage.

It appears we leave no stone unturned. Even in death they are a part of our lives as we place stones on the graves of our loved ones.

We are deeply connected with stones. They are a part of our individual and collective mythologies, from the oldest stories of creation to the Rolling Stones and beyond.

Rolling Stones

You probably know the Greek myth of Sisyphus. He was a king who was deceitful, clever, abusive, and cheated everyone from Zeus to Death. Finally he crossed the Gods once too often and they gave him a punishment that would last throughout eternity.

He would be forced to roll a heavy stone almost to the top of a steep hill only to watch it slip from his grasp and roll back down to the bottom, where he would have to begin again.

This myth has captured the imagination of the likes of Franz Kafka and Albert Camus, of philosophers, artists, writers, and literati for centuries. The evil king has even become an adjectival icon: meaningless tasks are described as Sisyphean.

One of the many interpretations of the myth has it that Sisyphus's never completed task represents a life made meaningless by mindless repetition. There is only the struggle, never completion.

I find that helpful for those of us in crisis because in our moments of despair we can identify! We can easily feel stuck. Like Sisyphus and his stone, we can feel doomed to the endless repetition of problems with the solution forever eluding us.

As noted in **R is for Remember** that is the time to stop rolling the stone and become still until we regain our perspective; still as a stone.

Especially in our Sisyphean moments, we need to remember that we can live creatively and consciously no matter what battles rage around us.

Stillness can be found in many ways. I'd like to offer two approaches here, both of which entail throwing stones. One is to hurl and toss, and the other to gently drop.

To make either one worthwhile, we need to shift our brains into a *relaxed* state. These two bring very different results, so pick the one you most need now.

First read through the text. Then close your eyes, relax your body and play it through. You can also record these and play them back at will.

Hurling stones

Despite our best intentions to rise above it all, when life is a rocky road (☺) we have some righteous rage.

111

That's fine, but we want to keep a fighting spirit, not suffer under misdirected anger.

Releasing anger helps strengthen our fighting spirit. This is a short exercise to permanently release issues. You can do it over and over with old and new challenges, wherever and whenever you have a few minutes to close your eyes and relax.

Nobody will know what you're doing, and you will feel much, much better when you open your eyes again.

In a relaxed state, go to the safe naturscape of your mind. Find a place to create a small hut or a cave with a low ceiling.

Know that once you enter you will find some sticky notes on the ceiling.

Written on each sticky note will be a few words that recall something that made you angry. It is something you don't want to keep carrying.

Notice too in one corner lie a pile of interesting looking stones.

Choose the sticky note with the issue you want to release and yank it down. Take it over to the stones and select one. Now touch the sticky note to the stone.

The two bond instantly and you are able to clearly see the message now carved into the stone.

Take the stone to the doorway. As you look out you'll see a big sky with a mountain range on the horizon. You know that when you throw this stone it will disappear forever over the mountains and far, far beyond, across the huge sky.

Your arm is infused now with the magical power of your anger. It is propelled by the intent of your most cherished dreams and transformed into a vastly stronger tool than you ever imagined.

Now with great ease you powerfully hurl the stone. You are fully alert as you watch.

Watch as it flies from your arm. Watch as it gets smaller and smaller. Watch as it disappears into nothingness over the distant mountains.

Knowing it is done, you now turn your back on the completed task. Gently bring yourself back, knowing the change is permanent.

If you choose, you can stay a while longer to repeat this with more sticky notes. Whenever you've had enough, return with a smile knowing you have accomplished a great deal.

Ultimately you will get all the notes off the ceiling, but for now there is no hurry.

Should a new insult or annoyance come your way simply break its bones by throwing sticky note stones.

Minding your own stones

This is a different, but equally powerful technique. Now instead of releasing what you don't want, this will help solidify and make part of you what you *do* want.

Take a walk in your mind. Go to your magical safe place. Make sure you are completely relaxed. In this fully relaxed state, walk over to a pond or lake. Create it as you wish.

Make it safe, beautiful, and easily accessible. It is important that your body of water has a shallow, sandy bottom you can wade into comfortably, and that the water there is completely clear.

Nearby you notice a pile of stones. They are beautiful!

They're brightly colored in all your favorite colors. Each has a word on it. It may be Love or Calm, Hope, or Peace. Look at the rocks and pick up the one that you need right now.

Notice how the letters of the word are etched into the brightly colored stone. Run your fingers over the letters. Roll the stone around in your hand. Explore it. Enjoy the stone as a child would.

When you are ready, take the stone and wade into the water. Wait and watch as the water again becomes still around you and it is clear and pristine.

Where you stand is secure, and the water is still and shallow. Right in front of you the water becomes quite deep, but so clear and calm that the sunlight offers you a perfect view right down to the deep, sandy bottom.

When all is completely still and you are ready, drop the stone into the clear, deep water and watch it float gently down to the bottom.

The colors are an array of beauty and the word is still clear to you even as the stone nestles into the sandy bottom.

Watch and wait as the water settles and the stone, with its shimmering word still clearly visible, seems comfortably settled in its new home.

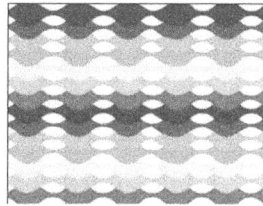

Leave knowing it will remain there always. You now realize this watery home is a deep part of you, for you have brought this new sense into the watery depths of your cells, your mind and your soul.

It is done and it feels wonderful.

Bless the water if you are so inclined. Repeat as often as you'd like.

You can feel good and smile. I assure you, you have just accomplished more and worked smarter, not harder, than in a long, perhaps very long, time.

Stonativities

❖ Look at Hurling Stones and Mind Your Own Stones; they are powerful stonativities. If you are so inclined you could make a recording of them in your own voice and come back to them at times of your choosing.

❖ Go to your naturscape and imagine yourself still, as still as a stone.

❖ Go to your naturscape and play with stones. Enjoy.

❖ If you're feeling like some handiwork might help, go to a river, the ocean, a woods or any place in nature that has meaning for you. Bring back a stone and paint it with a letter or a sign or an image that brings you peace or a smile.

Consider it your pet stone.

T is for Trust

"No soul is desolate as long as there is a human being for whom it can feel trust and reverence." **T.S. Eliot,** (American-born playwright and poet, 1888-1965)

As I've mentioned, T R U S T is a major biggie. I often mention it because so much of our ability to cope flows from its presence or lack thereof.

Sure it helps to have someone remind you to 'Let it be,' 'Let go, let God,' 'Trust the universe,' or whatever equivalent resonates with you. It helps for a while.

Then the old familiar fears, anxieties and worries kick in. I offer this chapter as a way to provide enduring help. It is broken down into two parts:

One: a challenge: Does it make sense to trust?

Two: If it makes sense to trust, how does a crisising person *actually trust* in the hardest of times?

You Fool!

Perhaps you are familiar with the Fool as depicted in the Tarot. At first blush, this guy looks like a complete idiot. Each deck draws the picture a little differently, but the theme is always the same.

There's a Pollyanna marching along, appearing to have not a care in the world, perky little dog at his feet. You can just imagine him (in most decks the Fool is male) whistling a happy tune.

The idiot, or more appropriately the Fool, is about to happily walk right off a cliff and into the abyss!

But ha and HA! The Fool always has a bag, like the one slung over his shoulder in this picture from the Rider-Waite deck. To all appearances it's just a poor man's few belongings.

And therein lays the mystery. What's really in the pack is a whole world of goodies waiting to be tried out. Think of them as the Fool's Tools.

The Fool is the Adventurer. He is T R U S T incarnate.

By most interpretations the entire numbered Tarot Deck are the Fool's experiences. The Fool is zero. He's got 21 learning experiences to go through until he reaches the Major Arcana card # 21 – The World.

By the time the Fool has completed all the experiences, the world is at his fingertips. His world is unlimited.

The real question about trust is this: Do you want to be a Fool? Do you want to view all this 'stuff' of life as experiences, or do you want to forget to remember all you are and all you can be and spend time in the past, in the future, and ultimately in either regret or worry.

Believe me, in no way am I diminishing the enormity of what you're coping with. Remember who's writing this, after all.

What I'm really saying is that trust is not blind hope and letting go. It *is* blind hope and it *is* letting go, but it is accompanied by trust in oneself.

We trust in the memory of the whole person we truly are. We trust that we will handle whatever comes at us and keep going.

Ultimately T R U S T is not trust in a superior being; it is trust in the superior being that we are.

With that belief, with Remembering (check out **R** if you haven't yet), trust becomes the center of the wheel, simply the natural approach to life's great challenges.

I want to trust. Now what?

Let's say we are in agreement that trust is a natural way to be in the world and that trust actually helps us cope with our challenges. Unless you're a natural at it trust will still take some doing.

More appropriately, it will take some remembering. We don't need to relearn, just remember.

As an approach to life, trust lies between "use it or lose it" and "you never forget how to ride a bicycle." It's like a muscle we need to keep exercising, but different because it won't atrophy through lack of use. It's still in us because it is part of our wiring.

Children have the Fool's trust naturally, but as adults we are expected to put that away along with our other toys. It's no wonder trust can feel like a challenge.

We are encouraged to manage, worry, and control. We are rewarded for micro-managing and doting. This makes it difficult to flex the trust muscle.

It could seem wimpy, as if we were unwilling to take control over our lives. At least that's the feedback we tend to get from the outside world -- spoken or not.

In the work world, as responsible adults, and even in our social lives we are generally expected to control and manage it all.

We are rarely supported for taking the time and making the effort to separate what we can control from what we cannot. This hodgepodge gets severely bollixed up in the depths of crisis and prone to lose what little perspective we may have had. Try out the Trust Two-step:

The Trust Two-Step

Step one: Unless you are a natural Fool, the first, best and most effective way to experience trust is through *gratitude, prayer, and meditation.*

You may know a different way or call it by a different name. But somehow we need to find a way to connect to something larger, more compassionate and more loving than ourselves.

If T R U S T is the Fool's house an open-hearted and grateful sense of well-being is the threshold we must cross to enter.

Being in that place is akin to the feeling of holding a puppy or a baby. Our hearts are open and the world feels right within and around us.

Step two: We need a repository to deposit all the things that are outside our control.

The 'worry basket' is a wonderful representation for this. In some Native American traditions people have worry baskets outside their homes.

When guests visit they drop in stones or twigs, as a representation of their worries. When they leave they take their worries with them, and either hand them back to nature or deposit them in the worry basket outside their own home.

I like that approach partly because no one keeps the worries. The implication is that most things we worry about can be tossed away or at least kept at bay. We may not be able to change or control them, but we can put them down or let them go.

Trustativities

❖ Remember trusting in an outcome and then having it fall into place? That's empowering! In your naturscape, go back there and mark that feeling in your body.

Recreate that physical feeling in a conscious state as often as possible. If you need to recapture it to make it strong again go back to your naturscape.

❖ Buy or make your own version of a worry basket and keep it outside your door. Drop off the day's worries whenever you walk in.

❖ Buy or make a box. Write a worry on a piece of paper and drop it in.

❖ Reflect on this: What Fool's Tools do you carry in your bag?

$\mathcal{U}$ is for Understanding

"Your pain is the breaking of the shell that encloses your understanding." – **Khalil Gibran** (Lebanese-American artist, poet, writer 1883-1931)

You may have wondered why this book has no section on forgiveness. It is well-known in religious and spiritual circles that forgiveness heals.

The general belief is this. When we carry anger it is we who suffer. When we forgive others we forgive ourselves and we set ourselves free. No argument from me.

Where I have concerns is with forgiveness itself. What is it? You may feel that you are generous of heart and large of spirit till the cows come home, but it would be a risky mistake to confuse that with forgiveness.

I believe there is no shortcut to forgiveness. There are essential prerequisites that must be met, and in my opinion, it's all about the pre-reqs.

As a hypnotherapist I have seen the damage when people 'forgive' too soon. The emotional wounds are still there, but they are buried deeper now and have become less accessible.

The only substantive change is a lack of awareness that real forgiveness has not yet taken place.

As bits of the old feelings bubble to the surface, they bring with them internal conflict and guilt. Premature forgiveness is as unsatisfying as other premature outbursts and liquids.

I find the term forgiveness so laden with subtexts that I prefer to use the term *understanding*. It feels nowhere near as complex as forgiveness. Instead it feels accessible to mere mortals.

Even more than its accessibility, full understanding brings awareness and is the top pre-req, the main move, the bee's knees, and the sine qua non of real forgiveness. Look at it this way.

You or the tiger?

Let's say you're about to exit the safety of your cave and a saber-toothed tiger jumps out at you. Aw snap! You retreat, the tiger stays. This gets you to thinking.

You are a pacifist cave dweller by nature, perhaps even a vegetarian. You do not easily take another life. Yet you come to a full awareness of your present situation:

This tiger is hungry and will not let you out of the cave without turning you into a happy meal. You research and gather together pieces of the puzzle. As you do so you organize the data and information at hand.

You must leave your cave to survive.

You have the means to kill the tiger.

The tiger meat will feed your family and the skin will keep you warm.

One of you must die for the other to live.

You must take action if you are to survive.

Viewed in a fuller context you accept that you and the tiger are really no different. Were you the tiger, you too would be out there pacing.

You decide to kill the tiger. Because you are a gentle soul, you offer a prayer of forgiveness for the life you take. You offer a prayer of gratitude for the life-supporting offerings you receive.

Now that's natural and the pieces all fall into place. Why? Because you have moved beyond your emotions and have come to fully understand the situation in its total context.

You have overcome the fear of death -- yours and the tiger's -- overcome your doubts, and have moved beyond anger. You freed yourself up to feel gratitude and forgiveness.

Indeed, forgiveness and gratitude are the logical result of understanding.

With understanding comes full awareness. You view the situation objectively and place it in its full context. When understanding replaces judgment and emotion, abundant gratitude and forgiveness are two of the low hanging fruits.

Chickens and eggs

Granted many of our challenges are not as simple as a tiger at the mouth of the cave. On the other hand, most of our challenges won't kill us either. They'll just rock our world, which brings me to why understanding is not more prevalent.

There's a bit of a chicken and egg thing going on.

In order to gain understanding we need distance and empathy. Ain't no other way. But it's counter-intuitive to believe we will find distance or empathy in a compost heap of Trouble.

So there we are in a troublesome and rather vicious circle unless we can find a way out.

I say if you can't figure out who's on first and what's on second, don't waste energy on it. Save it for what you can figure out.

Therefore, Terra's first law of understanding is...

126

CHILL! Like the man said, 'don't sweat the small stuff.'

Take a deep breath. Relax. Then do whatever you need to take just one step back from the whole mess. It can be through creating worst case scenarios, reframing, broadening the picture or considering it odd.

When you want to get a better understanding you've got to take a step back first. Even a small one.

A clean slice through the Gordian knot of complexity and you gain just enough objectivity to assess what's really going on. You haven't changed anything yet, but you have placed yourself in position to do so.

That distance is essential! It's like pixels on a computer. Zoom in and it's just a bunch of tiny boxes. Zoom out and the image takes on shape, form and depth.

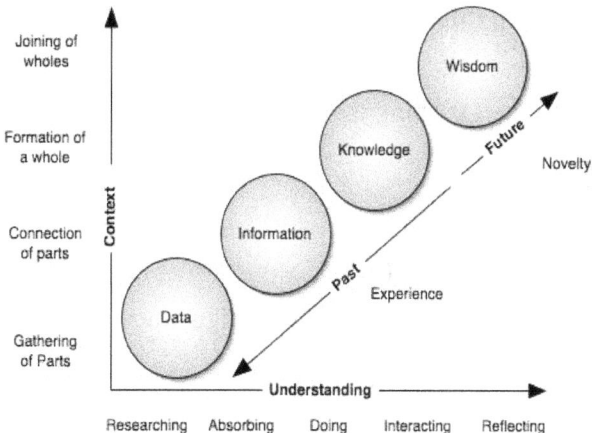

This theory is based on the work of Harlan Cleveland (1982), and places understanding on a continuum.

The vertical axis is *Context*, which moves from separateness to gathering and piecing together and ultimately joining all the pieces into a coherent whole.

The horizontal axis is *Understanding*. It goes through action steps such as research, absorbing and reflection.

Create some breathing space between you and your issue and for the moment, that's all you need.

When it comes to understanding, the first step forward is that one step back.

True understanding may take not only some distance so you can reframe, but rethinking based on some hard work, diligence, or research on your part.

It may entail talking to others in a new way, asking different questions and being open to unexpected answers. Understanding isn't handed to you, it is gained. It's not free; it's earned.

By combining a more complete context with increasing levels of understanding we move up and out from data to information, through knowledge and ultimately to wisdom.

And why is it worth all that effort? It is because true understanding is personal freedom.

I can't say what it will do for others involved in your issue. Placing people and events in a full context and moving to wisdom in our interpretations of their actions may or may not impact them in a positive way. One thing I am certain of though.

When we really understand an issue, we also set in motion what is needed for deep, true and permanent forgiveness.

In so doing we have gifted ourselves with the mental and emotional freedom we desperately need to cope with crisis.

Understandativities

❖ Find an issue, concern or worry that you would like to work with. Where are you on the understanding continuum?

❖ Can you use research and information-gathering to pull the pieces together? How would that look?

❖ If you have an issue you don't 'understand,' how would you create enough emotional distance to start along the path of a fuller understanding?

❖ What is the first step you would take?

V is for Village

"Lars asked us not to wear black today.... From her wheel-chair, Bianca reached out and touched us all, in ways we could never have imagined. She was a teacher. She was a lesson in courage. And Bianca loved us all. Especially Lars. Especially him." **"Lars and the Real Girl"** (2007 Oscar-nominated film about the impacts on a small town when a socially inept young man develops a relationship with a life-sized doll named Bianca.)

Village life... Does the thought get your juices flowing with fantasies of neighboring huts and built-in child care? Or does it feel like a backwoods lifestyle that would bore you to death?

Whichever side you come down on, the evolutionary facts remain. We are group animals and the village is a natural lifestyle for us humans.

When a Big Upheaval hits, we need a village to help us out, although through the narrow lens of our pain and suffering we may not readily notice its importance in our lives.

Statistically speaking, beware

According to recent studies, the importance of a support system can hardly be overestimated. Even if the support system is not physically present, it still helps. These same studies note that support impacts our

health, sense of well-being and even longevity.
(http://www.nytimes.com/2009/04/21/health/21well.html?_r=1)

Such studies are helpful, but I have a caveat. If you are in crisis, you may well be looking at the statistical outcomes for folks in your situation. This is probably most true for health crises, but the impacts are there for other types as well.

While studies are guideposts, they deal with people in the abstract. They gather important data but that holds *no* direct correlation to any *single* individual.

When I was diagnosed with stage three breast cancer I had access to any number of statistical likelihoods about my future. I chose to ignore them all.

If X number of women with my diagnosis died within Y years and T number were cured, it still held no answers for me.

No study and no amount of data could predict what would happen to me. The same is true with support.

If you never reach out during your crisis and have no friends, no family and live only to read books like this one, the data still says nothing about you personally.

That said, I do want to point out the advantages of the village. In mine live three clans: one of professionals;

another of friends, family and loved ones; and a third filled with activities that replenish me.

Every chapter in this book belongs to, comes from, or is inspired by one of those clans.

I had a strong belief that I would heal from cancer. I based it on a lot of factors, including trust in my clans. Mostly though, it came from self-knowledge about the needs of my own body, mind, and spirit. This is true for you too.

With self-knowledge and trust you can access what you need for success, even from a life situation you would rather not be in.

Yours to win... or lose

My village didn't fall from the sky and a good one won't for you either. Your village is yours to nurture and maintain. Ah, but once organized and nurtured the rewards flow back to you for a lifetime.

You are the driver of the bus, the captain of the ship, the pilot of the plane and chief engineer on the train. You, Number One, are the one and only.

I was privileged to have fabulous insurance and to be in one of the best longitudes and latitudes for cancer care. Still, if I had not put out the effort I would have gone through the standard medical machinery without other essential support. I knew that was not healthy for me.

The triple clan village

One:

I knew that living in a whirlwind of doctors, hospitals and allopathic treatments would have sucked the spirit out of me as sure as any dementor Harry Potter faced.

I definitely needed a Patronus spell to feed my soul.[1]

To supplement western medicine I pulled out my wand and made use of every eastern, metaphysical and magical support that felt right. Acupuncture, hypnotherapy, shamanic doctoring, herbs, and qigong were big parts.

That entire group of professionals was my first clan.

---

[1] For all you muggles – the dementors destroy humans by destroying hope. They create utter despair and, steal the soul. Summoned with a powerful incantation, the Patronus is a shimmering protector that emerges as an animal from the tip of the wand. It never despairs, but is filled with light and hope. Dementors must flee from them or be destroyed. (Now is that a cool metaphor or what!)

Two:

I knew that I would not benefit from something that is highly recommended and has great success – statistically speaking. Cancer support groups have been manna for many patients. For me it was the opposite.

I needed positive input and I needed heroes. I thrived on hope and giggles, love and warmth and on the stories of amazing women who had been through worse and survived.

 I sought out the support of those friends and family members who understood what I needed. I basked in it and postponed other contacts for another time.

Those interpersonal relationships were my second clan.

Three:

I also loved being around the energy of young people, the adoration of dogs, and the independence of cats.

I thrived on images of the ocean, walks in the woods, the sun, and stories of mermaids, sea horses and Goddesses. I watched funny movies and revenge movies filled with gratuitous violence.

I spent quality time in the gentle centering movements of qigong. I made a point of listening supportively to other people's non-health related interests.

I lost myself in journaling, in my work, and in modeling my healing for others. I read myths and tales of good spirits. I took on art projects, drew and doodled.

That state of being and of doing was my third clan.

Altogether life in the village was good.

Intention

I recommended the same method for those coping with non-health related crises. All Big Crises weaken under the enormous weight of a Powerful Village, which is not just the one that happens to surround us or that we were born into.

The big stuff requires an *intentional* village. Intent is the most powerful tool you can have for self-empowerment. Self-doubt and negativity have no place in the creation of a village.

With intention as your tool, create your village through self-worth, self-knowledge, and a desire for personal transformation.

The questions below are designed as a guide to getting started. Find answers to these questions, create your village, and I promise you will not only get through the dark nights of your crisis with the support you need.

You will be a happier, more confident and more successful person on the sunny days of the other side.

Villativities

❖ What professionals are available for help? When it comes to professional support you do the hiring. Interview them. Go for second opinions. Don't stop till you have the best.

❖ Who is poisonous for you? Even if it's a family member or close friend avoid them like the plague during this time. Let them know you will be back, but this is your time to heal.

❖ Who supports you? Nurture those relationships.

❖ What is a balm to your spirit? Build it into your life. Don't take no from yourself or anyone else.

❖ What free time activities do you take part in to help yourself? Do them religiously.

❖ What else might be of interest to you? Make the effort to seek it out. It may seem like the wrong time, but now *is* the time.

w is for Wonder

Daisy: *What kind of a garden do you come from?*
Alice: *Oh, I don't come from any garden.*
Daisy: *Do you suppose she's a wildflower?*
"Alice's Adventures in Wonderland" 1865 by **Lewis Carroll** (English author, mathematician, photographer, logician, inventor 1832-1898)

There's the ponderous pondering verb wonder as in *"I wonder how in the hell I ever got into this mess."*

There's the noun wonder that waves at us from our rear view mirrors as in: *"It's a wonder you ever survived that one honey!* Or *"It's a wonder someone as* (insert negative of choice) as *you ever managed to* (insert an achievement or success)!"

That's negative back talk you really don't need right now. Like Patrick Swayze pestering Whoopi Goldberg in *Ghost*, these kinds of wonder can haunt us. They are a fast track to nowhere.

Wonder with a capital W

The wonder I'm interested in is rare and delicate. Like many childhood joys it is fragile, easily lost, and difficult to reclaim.

It's worth the battle to hold on to though and if necessary, the fight to regain it, because without it life becomes no more than a series of repetitions.

Instead of learnings and insights we get predictable outcomes. Mediocrity replaces excitement and clarity. We may well end up satisfied with sitting in the back seat as life drives us around in circles.

As a Go master famously cautioned his student, we can keep a sense of freshness and wonder about us as we gain 20 years of experience, or we can experience one year, repeated 20 times.

Wonder is stolen from us when we are in crisis. It is one of the great losses because that is when we need it most.

Viewing the world around us with wonder is a secret to coping. It helps us problem solve and is a key to finding fresh answers to old dilemmas. Especially in a Big Crisis we must take on the battle and reclaim our right to see life through our eyes of wonder.

A Zen Tale

A famous Zen parable tells of a learned professor who repeatedly petitioned a master to become his student. After many unsuccessful attempts, the master finally opened the door and invited the professor inside for tea.

The master gracefully poured tea into his guest's cup. He poured until the tea overflowed the cup, then the saucer, spilled onto the table and finally onto the angry professor's lap.

The professor jumped up screaming that the master was crazy.

"Perhaps," he acknowledged, "but I cannot teach you anything. Your mind is like this teacup. It is so full that nothing more can get in."

Beginner's mind

The master was telling him he lacked 'beginner's mind.' He had no room for newness; he had lost his sense of wonder.

Beginner's (or baby's) mind is the opposite. It is empty and open, aware yet relaxed. This mind enjoys a stroll and tackles challenges with the same sense of wonder and excitement.

From that state of mind, creativity flows outward and solutions to difficulties slip inward.

From social experiments to scientific examination, there is a growing body of evidence to back up the importance of our state of mind as we interpret – and impact – the world around us.

In a real sense, all things change when we do.

Twenty thousand times

Assume we accept the importance of approaching life with wonder and using beginner's mind. Acceptance doesn't necessarily make it easy.

It may be easy to change how we approach life and its dramas occasionally or in certain instances. But incorporating that into our lives in lasting ways needs practice. As my martial arts teacher would say: "Twenty thousand times."

We need help for that kind of lasting change, especially in rough times. Hence a book such as this, filled with bits of wit and wisdom. The methods I offer are tried and tested, and they work.

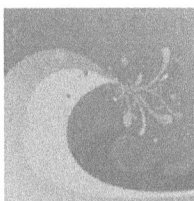

The next chapter will help you find your own silver bullet to permanent change. Until then, I want to offer another Japanese concept that may help.

Throughout my many years of martial arts study I was intrigued by 'shin.'

Heart and mind together

Despite its profound, universal simplicity and applicability, shin is untranslatable into English.

Shin is a state of being that can be applied anywhere, combining as it does an open, loving heart with our best mental state. My teacher often referred to shinpa – the waves of shin.

Perhaps the closest translation for shinpa is good vibes. I offer shinpa as my most readily accessible tool for change.

You can use shinpa briefly a thousand times a day. A little body trigger can serve as a reminder.

Cope with the Big Crisis with shinpa. Get through the rough patches with shinpa. Use it to create the mood that connects you with the change you want to become. Let the good vibes roll.

Do these wondertivities and you'll notice an immediate sense of well-being. Keep at them and they will catalyze your life with excitement freshness, and a vital life energy.

Wondativities

❖ Wherever you are right now take a moment and look around. Focus on one object and note what thoughts, ideas or feelings arise.

Now shift into 'beginner's mind.' Look at that object as if you have never seen it before. Look at it as if it is the very first time.

What changes?

❖ Look at an object and note your thoughts or feelings. Now apply shinpa. Look at the object with your best mind and an open heart.

What changes?

❖ Once you have shifted into a state of being you like, either beginner's mind or shinpa, use a little body movement or touch while you are in that state. This will be your 'trigger' to recall that state whenever you choose.

A reminder about triggers: This is a small physical movement, like rubbing two fingers together, that is connected to an experience you want to recall.

It creates an abiding association that is a bridge between your body and the experience. With practice you can use the movement and the experience comes flowing in.

✗ is for ?, the X-Factor

"I've failed over and over and over again in my life and that is why I succeed." **Michael Jordan** (philanthropist, businessman, former professional basketball player, considered one of the greatest players of all time.)

The **X-factor** is the great unknown. It is the part I can't know or intuit. Neither can anyone else – except you. I can write about coping with crises, give you examples and options, but unless something resonates with you, it is for naught.

This ABC book was designed to offer tips, activities and ideas to help stimulate your imagination and suggest ways to help you cope with any Big Crisis you face now or may face in the future.

I have created Chapter **X** to help ensure that when you walk away from this book you don't leave empty handed. After all, we're very close to **Z**, and our time together is drawing to a close.

So this is where you step into the book as your own author, my X-factor friend.

This is not an exam and I'm not expecting to see the results – although that would be fun. **X** is your letter, and my goals are simple:

✓ Help you find, remember, deepen or renew what spoke to you in this book

✓ Help you clarify why that stood out for you.

✓ Provide a forum for you to create an activity that brings resolution and healing right to your doorstep.

X = You. It's a blank until you make of this letter what you will.

Please feel free to draw, scribble, write with your non-dominant hand... whatever allows you to really chew on this and make it your own.

It's nothing yet. Go ahead and make something of it.

My favorite letter was: _____

*I liked/loved it because:*_____
_____

(for example: it changed my perspective, I got new info, I smiled)

*The thought of this idea really upset me because:*_____
_____

And here's what I intend to do about it: _____

_____

*What I'm going to most remember from this book is:*_____

_____

*My favorite activity was:*_____

_____

*Because I:*_____

_____

In flipping back through the alphabet just now, this caught my attention: _____

_____

Because: _____

_____

If I were to select only one activity it would be:

_____

If I were to change one attitude or undertake only one activity to improve my mental state it would be:

_____

_____

*If I were to change one attitude or undertake only one activity to garner more support as I cope with this crisis, it would be:*_____

_____

I've already begun doing this for my mental state:

_____

_____

Color the star for that!

I've already begun doing this to help me cope more easily: _____

_____

A star to you for that as well!

I am deeply grateful that: _____
_____

Now it's freestyle. Take time for additional reflection, ideas, rants, raves, dreams......

Y is for Yes!

"The world's a playground. You know that when you are a kid, but somewhere along the way everyone forgets it." **Yes Man** (2008 American comedy about a man who changes his life by saying Yes to everything. Stars Jim Carrey and Zooey Deschanel)

We know how quickly things in our private lives can fall apart when a Big Hit slaps us down. That's bad enough; it's even worse when the world around us feels like it's coming unglued, and we can only stand there looking in from the outside.

It can feel like we are in a world made of No's. Feeling denied, we can easily begin to measure all things through the stresses, strains, and wants that fill our lives.

No longer smiling as we remember the good times, we can instead be filled with teary nostalgia. Through the rubble of our current existence, things that were horrible at the time can start smelling like a rose by comparison.

Things like health or work, a home, financial security or true love can feel like it is only for others, and never again will be ours. NO becomes the opportunity traffic cop whistle blowing, hand raised.

Paraphrasing Gandolf the Wizard, the world is slamming down its magic wand and telling us we shall not pass!

Bottom of the barrel

If you are in that No abyss, you have lost your life-sustaining sense of hope and your dreams.

Concepts like gratitude and trust are a foreign language. From the No world, life is at its bleakest.

When every opportunity feels like an exit and we are the ones summarily kicked out, this is the lowest point in a crisis. So take heart it won't get any worse. You've reached rock bottom and you can only go up from there.

Not everyone even gets there. Some people are able to ready themselves for battle even at the darkest of times and keep hope alive.

In my case, in the beginning of weeks of diagnosis hell I experienced a seemingly bottomless pit of anxiety, worry, powerlessness and negativity that was new, unexpected, and left me feeling unable to find my way out of the labyrinthine world of No.

I have worked with clients in protracted crisis where the bottom fell out from one day to the next. I asked of them what I asked of myself. What or who is really saying No? We all found the same answer.

Sure, there was a lot of No going around. But that was not the source of the misery. The bottom falls out if we incorporate No beyond the circumstances of our lives and *into the person we believe we have become.*

Once we refuse to see ourselves as the poor little No girl or boy everything shifts. Our outer world can still be a shambles and our future uncertain, but we no longer are.

No more No girls and boys

How did I turn it around? How did my clients? By using all the techniques I have written about in this book. By finding what speaks to us as unique individuals. Some rely more on the Village, others on Trust or Gratitude, Remembering or Understanding.

These allow us to walk right through those unwelcoming walls of No into an astoundingly welcoming and un-complicated world.

From there, loss looks different. Instead of asking how we can survive we ask ourselves what we truly need right now. What helps me thrive now? How can I be the beautiful lotus that rises from mud?

By asking the right questions we move from victim to problem-solver.

*When we stop asking how we will survive in the future and focus on how we can thrive **now**, we walk through walls and enter a welcoming world.*

Yes I could

The 2008 presidential election was historic in that we would have either a woman or a non-white in office for the first time. Despite deep political divisions, the country was riveted.

With few exceptions, Americans were touched by the sense of history surrounding Barack Obama and the story of his 'improbable journey.'

By all predictions his life should have gone in an entirely different direction. Logic dictated that even if he ran for President in 2008 he would never, ever win. But there he was, and here we are.

One day on a stump speech candidate Obama spoke his opinion of those who thought his quest was too Quixotic and who claimed the country was not ready, of all those who said: "No!"

His simple answer of "Yes!, yes we can" became a refrain of hope that echoed through hearts and spirits, blasted away obstacles, and ultimately made history.

He created a world of Yes!, not only for himself, but for a nation. With the power of Yes! He had already broken innumerable glass ceilings until smashing the tallest to become President.

I am not speaking politically here; I am speaking of a personal and social phenomenon that turned into a movement and swept him into office. I am speaking of the colossal power of **Yes!**

Yes!ativities:

❖ Do the No's outweigh the Yes!es in your life?

❖ If you have No's in your life, consider writing down the source. Forcing clarity sometimes takes care of it right there.

❖ Can you find any self-imposed limitations as you move through your crisis?

❖ What can you do to turn blocks and no's into Yes!es? Brainstorm. Then commit your ideas to writing or create an action plan or chart. Place your action plan front and center of your mind and eyes.

❖ What are you lacking in your life *right now* at this very moment?

Z is for Zowie!

"And Charlie, don't forget about what happened to the man who suddenly got everything he ever wanted. He lived happily ever after." (From "Charlie and the Chocolate Factory," **Roald Dahl**, British writer 1916 – 1990)

Did you reach Zowie! in 26 steps? If you have made it this far and are not there yet, rest assured you will. The truth is that during my Big One I had some Zowie! moments, but not many.

I felt if I hit a Zenlike calm, if I could live in the moment and appreciate the love around me, if I could still laugh sometimes and kid around once in a while, if my heart melted when I saw my kids and leaped when a deer jumped across my path with amazing grace, if I cared about the sufferings and joys of others, if I could still smile at a stranger, well I figured if I could do those things then I was in the zone.

For then, it was good. It was enough. Once in a while I felt like king of the mountain and had a Zowie! moment and that was a freebie!

But Zowie! moments for those in crisis tend to come more after the fact, that is to say after resolution. And they keep on coming. Zowie! The sun seems to shine more fully in retrospect. It's what happens in if you've done your homework during the major crisis, the boarding school from hell.

I learned so much both during my journey through cancer and from those who I helped with their crises. I suspect that if you were drawn to this book you are on a similar learning trajectory.

If so, I'll tell you this:

You will prevail. It will be over. You will not only be able to cross the Big One off your list, you'll begin to write it in your mind in small letters.

No matter how hard the struggle, no matter how fragile you may feel during a crisis, you always, always have the potential to come out better.

I didn't say unscathed, I said better. If you're a grown-up you already know you won't get out of this world unchallenged. As Hank Williams sang: "No matter how you struggle and jive, you'll never get out of this world alive."

Scars never killed anyone. It's what we make of them that can either be deadly or help us become more passionate, sensitive, and caring.

Zowie! lays claim to victory, scars be damned.

Like enlightenment, it's unclear when Zowie! will hit. Like quality chocolate, one bite and an array of flavors burst out!

Also like good chocolate, Zowie! comes with a smile.

OMG, I survived and I'm a better person for it. *Zowie!*

I love my life because I knew I could and now I know I can. *Zowie!*

I want to contribute to others. I want to be of service and help, because I know what down looks like. *Zowie!*

I get to up a lot faster now. *Zowie!*

Zen in the art of Zowie!ism

Zowie! is dessert. Granted the main course sucks, but that makes dessert even tastier. Speaking for myself, I am not so enlightened that I live in a state of Zowie! I'm working on it though, and quien sabe, maybe someday.

If you've come through those dark times with tools in hand, you know you will cope with whatever may come down the pike at another time.

You know by now you can't control what or when that may be, but you also know you don't have to because you will find your way.

I say to those unknown and future challenges that you are no more than the unpredictable experiences of life. You may come, but you are not facing a novice.

We have looked our monsters in the eye and told them in no uncertain terms that we are bigger and better than they.

We now carry inside a toolbox of support, fortitude and resilience. We are the Fools who have marched through these 26 steps and if we need to again, why we'll just leapfrog through them.

My hope is that that you are able to call on your Zen self as you go through your paces, and when you're ready to get out there again and play in the sandbox that you do it with lots and lots of Zowie!

Zowativity

❖ Close the book and go play!

Bibliography

Beck, Martha. **Steering by Starlight: Finding Your Right Life No Matter What!** New York, NY: Rodale, Inc., 2008.

Bristol, Claude M. & Sherman, Harold. **TNT: The Power Within You.** Saddle River, N.J: Prentice Hall, 1987.

Cleveland, Harlan. "Information as Resource," *The Futurist,* December, 1982 p. 34-39

Clinton, Hillary Rodham. **It Takes A Village: And Other Lessons Children Teach Us.** New York, NY: Touchstone, Simon & Schuster, 1996.

Jung, Carl Gustav. **The Archetypes and The Collective Unconscious.** New York, NY: Routledge, 1991.

Murphy, Joseph. **The Power of Your Subconscious Mind.** Radford, VA: Wilder Publications, 2007.

Reps, Paul & Nyogen, Senzaki, ed. **Zen Flesh Zen Bones: A Collection of Zen and Pre-Zen Writing.** Boston, MA: Tuttle Publishing, 1998.

TERRA MAR, M.A., ChT has been involved in wellness and holistic healing throughout her adult life.

Her studies include meridian massage, yoga, aromatherapy, alchemical hypnotherapy and alchemical healing. She trained in a traditional martial art under a 10th degree master for over three decades, and holds a 7th degree black belt. She also is a certified Soaring Crane qigong teacher.

Her cancer diagnosis and treatment deepened her commitment to help others as they go through difficult times.

She has studied and used herbs for over two decades. Terra developed an extraordinary interest in rainforest herbs after trips to Costa Rica and Brazil. In 2007, she followed her passion for plants and planetary healing and began her own company, www.OnePlanetHerbs.com and a sister informational site www.herbalremedies-info.com. **OnePlanet Herbs** specializes in herbal tinctures that Terra produces from Amazon rainforest herbs.

Her first book, *ABC's of Natural Healing* takes a holistic approach to our role in Nature and in healing ourselves and the planet. It introduces Amazon rainforest herbs from a uniquely personal perspective.

Terra is available for seminars and personal coaching. Contact her at terra@oneplanetherbs.com